Thomas of Celano's
FIRST LIFE
of
St Francis of Assisi

Thomas of Celano's
FIRST LIFE
of
St Francis of Assisi

Translated by
CHRISTOPHER STACE

TRIANGLE

Published in Great Britain in 2000 by
Society for Promoting Christian Knowledge
Holy Trinity Church
Marylebone Road
London NW1 4DU

British Library Cataloguing-in-Publication Data

A catalogue record for this book is available from the
British Library

ISBN 0-281-05245-X

Typeset by Pioneer Associates, Perthshire
Printed in Great Britain by
Caledonian International, Glasgow

CONTENTS

LIST OF ILLUSTRATIONS

INTRODUCTION

St Francis of Assisi – what a host of images the name conjures: films, novels, biographies, paintings, colleges, seminaries, and even streets and cities. One image I see before me now: an emaciated, weasel-faced monk peering tiredly from beneath a brown cowl; a skeletonic, ascetic, mystical, romantic, other-worldly figure with a straggly beard on his long, thin face, his complexion sallow, his brow lined and furrowed. His eyes brim with tears, his eyebrows are raised in a manner that suggests patience and humility and suffering. The bony fingers of his left hand hold a book (presumably a Gospel), while he shows the palm of his right hand to the viewer in a gesture indicative of humility and resignation. In the middle of his right palm and on the outside of his left hand are large, bloody weals with blackened centres. He is displaying the stigmata, the marks of the crucifixion of Christ, which appeared on his body in the mountain hermitage of La Verna. The scarlet leather cover of his book bears the legend VERA SANCTI FRANCISCI EFFIGIES, 'the true likeness of St Francis'.

Is this the legendary *Poverello*, the 'poor little man'? Almost certainly not. The portrait I possess is seventeenth-century, probably Spanish, a half-length figure done on copper; the background is bright gold, and the artist has given Francis a gloriously ornate halo. Gold and halo apart, perhaps, this is probably what most people imagine Francis looked like; yet it hardly agrees with the detailed word-picture given us by Thomas of Celano in his *First Life* (see Paragraph 83).

Nor does the painting in the Sacro Speco of Subiaco, which is believed by some to be the earliest portrait of the saint. It is dated 1223 and shows a severe but very serene, cowled monk with large, kindly eyes; his lips, however, are far from thin, and thin is what our author assures us they were.

A little-known portrait in the church of St Francis at Montefalco, about 12 miles south of Assisi, depicts a haloed monk (again with a scarlet book in his left hand) wearing a brown habit with white girdle; his head is tilted as it were in sorrow and humility. The Francis painted by the thirteenth-century 'St Francis Master' is one of ascetic sternness; he has a long, grim Byzantine face which is heavy-boned and well fleshed out. He almost sulks. Cimabue (c. 1240–1302) painted a Francis in the Lower Basilica at Assisi who is both human and realistic. This is a saint with a shaggy, homely face: it knows suffering, certainly, but it could break quickly into a smile. Here is 'a man of joyous aspect', as Celano puts it. But again his lips are not thin and his nose is not straight (as Celano tells us explicitly that they were: see Paragraph 83).

In his celebrated fresco-cycle in the Upper Basilica at Assisi, Giotto (1266/7–1337) sets out to show Francis as the heroic Christian saint, gloriously radiant, austere and dignified. This is no doubt the most authentic pictorial version of the stories told of St Francis. And Giotto's is an entirely new artistic language, with its intense concentration on character, its dramatic play of light on face and form. Here are real flesh-and-blood human beings, rounded figures of weight and substance taking part in events of immense significance.

But perhaps the most immediately human and memorable Francis of all is that in the portrait attributed to Simone Martini in the Lower Basilica of Assisi, dated 1317. Here is a glowing, haloed monk with an elongated, hypersensitive face and the most delicate features; he has a thin beard and a very long, straight nose. One can sense his compassion and sanctity, but equally certainly he lacks the essential dynamism of the real Francis.

Benozzo Gozzoli, working more than a century after Giotto's death, painted a cycle of frescoes depicting the life of the saint in the church of St Francis in Montefalco. He has a much lighter touch than the St Francis Master. His palette shows his lively appreciation of the natural world, and the Francis he creates is immediately appealing: here is an approachable, personal saint, the sort who would look and feel most at home in the villages and hill towns of Umbria.

Clearly, if we are to trust the words of Thomas of Celano (who after all knew Francis well, and when describing his physical features had no reason to tell anything but the truth) none of the extant portraits is definitive. But of course, just as every painted portrait indicates the artist's perception of his subject and his reasons for painting it, so every written portrayal reveals the same about its author. Celano wrote his *First Life* in haste at the Pope's command in order to justify the canonization of Francis, and the modern reader must bear this constantly in mind. How much, in fact, does it matter what Francis looked like? Surely it is far more important to know what he said and did. And for both we have to go back to Thomas of Celano.

The bare facts are these: Francis was born the son of a comfortably off merchant in the Umbrian town of Assisi in 1181. In his youth he was like any other youth – easy-going, pleasure-seeking and irresponsible. A prolonged illness changed him, and subsequently he underwent a complete conversion. Gradually, like-minded men gathered around him to live the gospel life and in 1209 or 1210 the Pope blessed him and approved the simple way of life he embraced, which was based on a few gospel sayings. From this grew the Order of Friars Minor. The Brotherhood was rigidly orthodox in its Catholic beliefs, but embraced utter poverty both collectively and individually; it was a mendicant order. Francis sent his friars away in twos on missions throughout Italy and beyond. A powerful preacher himself, he travelled indefatigably, and tried unsuccessfully to evangelize the Muslims in Palestine.

The Order was fast growing, however, and Francis was no administrator. Somewhere between 1217 and 1220 he resigned as Vicar and retired to La Verna, his hermitage high in the central Apennines not far from Arezzo. There, on 14 September 1224, he became the first human to receive the stigmata, the marks of Christ's passion, on his body. As Dante put it: 'On the rough crag twixt Tiber and Arno he received the last seal from Christ, which his members bore for two years' (*Paradiso*, Canto XI 106–8). He died in 1226 and was canonized only two years later.

Francis was a unique human being, a soaring spirit: though he is remote from us in time, he remains a saint for today. One of the great pleasures of writing this book has been to see the smile of familiarity, the look of instant recognition on the faces of friends when I answer their question, 'What are you writing?' Francis is a people's saint.

He was born into a world of conflict, an Italy torn between empire and papacy. Francis was only 16 when the people of Assisi ejected the imperial governor from his stronghold, the Rocca. And with the governor, interestingly, went the young boy of four who was to be the Emperor Frederick II, the *stupor mundi*. A more piquant contrast is scarcely imaginable: the almost insanely ambitious Emperor of the Holy Roman Empire and King of Sicily, the great warrior-diplomat who was to preside over the most cultivated court in Europe and finally be branded by his enemies as antichrist: and the *Poverello*, who despised himself, who longed to be poorer than the poor, who blazed with love and drew men to him, whose spiritual insight was to change the face of medieval Europe and to spark off a movement which has resonated through every century after.

And not only did Francis found his own Order of Friars Minor: he enabled the Poor Clares to develop so that women could live the contemplative life in enclosure in the spirit of poverty. They were linked with the Brothers and were eventually called the Second Order. For women and men, married or single, priests or lay to live the gospel life in their own setting, the Third Order was subsequently developed. And the members of this Third Order, the Tertiaries, pacifists living lives of honesty and purity, were in fact to challenge the whole feudal system, and make a vital contribution to the regeneration of medieval society.

Francis' influence, whether on his own times or on posterity, is hard to exaggerate. But if we cannot be sure of finding the real saint in his portraits, how can we come close to him today? Of course, we can see something of his ideals in practice in the three great orders of his vast family: in the *Conventuals* (who wear a black tunic with a white rope girdle, with a black cape and cowl, though currently the black tunic is changing to grey); in the *Friars Minor* (who wear a dark chestnut-brown habit and white rope girdle with a cowl hanging from a short cape); and in the bearded *Capuchins* (who wear a dark chestnut-coloured habit with a long pointed cowl). They all observe poverty, humility and obedience.

But where can we capture something of the authentic spirit of the *Poverello*, and separate the simple, gentle, meek soul from the industry that has grown up around his name? Not in tourist-packed Assisi with its beetling basilica; nor at the Portiuncula, once so tiny and intimate, now part of the sprawling baroque church of Santa Maria degli Angeli, the mother church of the Order. Nor even at lovely La Verna, where digital watches peep from brown sleeves as the beleaguered Brothers brave hordes of holidaymakers clicking their cameras at the Della Robbia altarpieces.

Then where? Francis can best be found, I think, in solitude and quiet amid the scenery he loved, in the hills and valleys of rural Umbria with their swathes of oak and ilex and ordered rows of vines and olives; in the valley of Rieti, especially, at the tiny shrines and chapels and villages that are saturated with his memory. At Poggio Bustone, where Francis had his vision of the future great-ness of his Order; or at Fonte Colombo where he dictated his revised rule to Brother Leo; or at the sacred spot near Greccio where Francis celebrated Christmas so memorably in 1223.

One must go back to the very beginnings and listen again to the barefoot tramp who preached the word of God so fervently and stirred men's hearts so profoundly; who preached directly and simply and swept away the cobwebs of apathy and neglect, the superstition and fear, the selfishness and pride of his people; who married Poverty, and 'their harmony and happy looks led men to love and wonder and sweet contemplation and holy thoughts' (Dante, *Paradiso*, Canto XI 76–8). First, one must go back to the saint's own writings; then to the *Life* written by his contemporary and disciple Thomas of Celano.

Celano's *Vita Prima*, the *First Life* of St Francis, was written at the command of Pope Gregory IX in 1228, two years after the saint's death. This explains the other name by which it is known – the *Legend of Gregory*. ('Legend' here implies nothing about the reliability of the material, but refers to the fact that it was composed to be read [Latin *legenda*] in friaries, like *The Golden Legend* compiled a generation later by the Dominican Jacopo da Voragine.) The *First Life* falls into three uneven parts: the first, comprising 30 chapters, deals with Francis' youth, his conversion, the founding of his Order, and his saintly life up to 1223, when he celebrated Christmas at Greccio. The second part is in ten chapters and describes the last two years of Francis' life, his stigmatization, and his death and burial; and the third part comprises two chapters (Paragraphs 119–51): one is an account of the canonization of Francis, and the other recounts some of the miracles he performed. The whole is subdivided carefully into 151 paragraphs, the first and last being respectively a prologue and epilogue.

We know too little of our author's life. He was born around AD 1185 in Celano in the Abruzzi, in the province of Aquila, about 80 miles south-east of Assisi. Some think he was already a priest when he joined Francis' Order in about 1215. He knew Francis intimately. He knew the saint as a friend; he understood the ideals which inspired him and which characterized the Brotherhood at its first beginnings. Subsequently, in 1221, he was sent on a mission to Germany where he served as Vicar Provincial of the Order, and he was still there a couple of years later. Then he seems to have gone back home to Italy. Though exactly how much contact he had with St Francis at the very end of his life is not known, his detailed account of Francis' canonization in 1228 strongly implies that he was himself an eyewitness at the great occasion. He states clearly in Paragraph 88 that from the penultimate year of Francis' life his account is based on the information he has been able to gather from other people. We know that Celano was living in Assisi in 1230, so it is reasonable to suppose that he would have been present at the translation of Francis' remains from St George's Church (where they had first been buried) to the magnificent new basilica that had been built in his honour.

In the years following the composition of the *First Life*, many new facts were discovered and many new things came to light about Francis that Celano had not been able to include. So in 1244 the new General of the Order, Crescentius of Iesi, asked Thomas to write a new Life of St Francis (known confusingly as the *Legenda Antiqua*, the 'Ancient Life', but generally referred to as the *Second Life*), and commanded all the friars to assist by submitting to him any relevant material they possessed concerning the life and miracles of the saint.

In his prologue to the *Second Life*, Celano speaks openly of his work as a collaboration. The bulk of this new biography, which is a supplement to, and not an alternative to, the *First Life*, was written between August 1246 and July 1247. In it Celano repeats some things, but he also adds new details.

Then, some years later, the Minister General appointed to succeed Crescentius of Iesi, John of Parma, asked Celano to write the *Treatise on the Miracles of Blessed Francis*. This work, composed between 1250 and 1253, concentrates on the miracles that occurred after the saint's death. The *First Life* in fact had listed only those miracles accepted and read out during the canonization process, and since the *Second Life* had only four paragraphs on appearances of St Francis to people after his death, clearly this did need further treatment. Though much in the *Treatise* is contained elsewhere, some 15 per cent of the material is new.

Among other things, Celano is also generally thought to have composed a *Legend of St Clare* written at the request of Pope Alexander IV and completed within eight years of the saint's death in 1253; and a *Legenda ad Usum Chori*, written about 1230, which is basically a concise version of the *First Life* but also contains interesting new material. And traditionally Celano has been regarded as the author of the *Dies Irae*.

Thomas of Celano died in around AD 1260, and today his body lies under the high altar of the monastery church of the Friars

Minor Conventual at Tagliacozzo, some 30 miles south-east of Rieti.

Celano based his *First Life* on his own personal knowledge and the evidence of 'reliable and trustworthy witnesses' (Prologue, Paragraph 1). In fact these witnesses must have provided the majority of his information. Celano could have consulted all the early followers and friends of Francis who were still living, Pope Gregory himself and indeed St Clare. He also refers frequently to the saint's own writings: the *Rules* he composed for his order, and his last will, called the *Testament* (which together are crucial for a proper understanding of Franciscan ideals); his various *Admonitions*; the *De Religiosa Habitudine in Eremo* in which he sets out the rules of life to be observed in small hermitages; and the *Canticle of Brother Sun*, the remarkable poem in which Francis praises the divine revelation in nature.

The *First Life*, however, is hardly biography as we know it today. For one thing, though Celano states that he will observe a rigid chronology to avoid confusion, he in fact does so only for the most important events, and not for things of lesser importance. For another, much of his narrative is simply hagiography. Like the Gospels, it is not written primarily to give accurate facts and dates, but to convey a message and a faith. Francis was Celano's hero and teacher: he was a saint, therefore Celano must show him to be a saint. (Francis in fact had his shortcomings and was well aware of them – something which is itself, of course, a sign of sanctity.) The *First Life*, then, sets out Francis' claim to sanctity, and Celano's climax, in which he rises to considerable literary heights, is the recognition of Francis' sanctity at his canonization. So we are given few details of, say, Francis' personal life or education: we are told nothing of the internal politics of the Order, or the day-to-day administration of the Brotherhood. In any case, such humdrum details would have been irrelevant to the author's purpose and out of place. What we do get is a vivid word-portrait of Francis' mind and heart, the heart of a poet, a visionary and an apostle.

Celano tells the truth as he sees it, the truth seen through the eyes of the thirteenth-century religious whose subject was his hero and idol. Some critics have accused him of inconsistency, pointing out his extraordinary bias in favour of Brother Elias wherever he is mentioned in the *First Life*, and his quite different attitude to Elias in the *Second Life*. The difference is certainly marked, but the discrepancy is easily explained. When Thomas wrote the *First Life* he saw Elias as a loyal friend of Francis and a distinguished Vicar General of the order; but subsequently he was to fall from grace for living in a manner contrary to the Franciscan ideal, and was eventually deposed and excommunicated. Other critics have taken exception to Celano's adulation of Gregory IX, but his admittedly rather fulsome praise is clearly sincere. Gregory was, after all, the Order's Protector, he was Francis' close friend, and, at the time of writing, he was the Pope.

The sincerity and honesty of the *First Life* can hardly be in doubt, and its historical value is not disputed. 'It is in fact', as Father Cuthbert wrote in 1914 in his seminal biography of the saint, 'the foundation upon which our critical knowledge of St Francis must be built up.' But of course for the fullest possible history of the saint we have to complete its partial picture with details from other writings – from Celano's own *Second Life*, for example, the so-called *Legend of the Three Companions*, and St Bonaventure's *Major Life*.

Celano is an erudite man, and reveals himself as a conscious and painstaking stylist. He can be allusive, occasionally even cryptic; he knows the Scriptures intimately and quotes them often; he knows the early Christian writers, too, and seems at home even with classical authors. Sometimes his fervour seems spontaneously to erupt and the result is an ejaculation of the most euphuistic piety, excessive by today's standards, but transparently sincere. His language is sometimes densely figurative; he loves contrasts and balanced phrases and clauses. He can hurry along at breathless speed with tiny, clipped sentences; then, when it suits him, he can be studiedly rhetorical and poetic. True to the fashion of his times, he secs allegorical meanings in almost everything. To enjoy Celano in full flow one could do no better than to read aloud his account of Francis' celebration of Christmas at Greccio (Paragraphs 84–7), or the process of canonization (Paragraphs 124–6).

Readers interested in the arts will instantly recognize many of the scenes described by Celano in paintings they know: 'the renunciation scene', for example, where Francis strips himself of his clothes before the Bishop of Assisi; 'Francis preaching before the sultan'; 'Francis preaching to the birds'; 'the Christmas crib at Greccio'; 'the stigmatization'. But they will also have seen many pictures of scenes not included in the *First Life*: 'the crucifix at St Damian's speaking to Francis' (telling him to 'rebuild my house'); 'Francis giving his clothes to a poor knight'; 'Francis producing water from a rock'; 'the dream of Innocent III' (that Francis would prop up his tottering Church). All these can be found in the *Second Life*. 'The taming of the wolf at Gubbio' is an incident in the charming collection of oral legends called *The Little Flowers of St Francis*; 'Francis predicting the death of a knight of Celano' comes from the *Treatise on the Miracles*, and is included in *The Golden Legend*. (*The Golden Legend*, which was finished by 1265, contains many anecdotes not in Celano's Lives, many of them strangely inconsequential, as well as repeating much of the same material.) And 'Francis' birth in a stable' between an ox and an ass comes from legend, pure and simple.

We are lucky to have Celano's Lives of St Francis at all. When St Bonaventure (who was elected Minister General of the Order in 1257) completed his *Major Life* of the saint in 1262/3, it was intended to replace all the existing Legends (the three works of Celano, plus several other short treatises which had appeared) and to give a consistent account of the life and acts of St Francis to a generation who had never known him. There was also dissension within the Order between the conservatives and the modernists (over, for example, the practice of poverty), and this new *Major Life* was an attempt to unite the Brotherhood. By this time there was a maze of material, none of it complete in itself, or constituting a homogeneous whole so, at the Chapter held in Narbonne in 1260, Bonaventure was asked to set matters straight with a new official Life, and at the Paris Chapter of 1266 it was decreed that all other Legends should be destroyed. This naturally had dire repercussions for the transmission of Celano's Lives. The Franciscans themselves appear to have obeyed the decree of the Chapter to the letter. But some 20 manuscripts did survive, several in Cistercian, and some in Benedictine monasteries, where scribes had wisely made their own copies.

Little can Francis have imagined what he had begun. Today the soaring, richly embellished basilica dominates his little home town and shouts his name to the world, a rich monument honouring the name of one who always wanted poverty and simplicity. Assisi is all Francis. He founded an Order which in 1211 numbered only about 300 brothers, but by the end of the century the figure had risen to many thousands. Franciscans came to England as early as 1224, and in the next 100 years had established no fewer than 50 houses with 1,350 friars.

The vision Francis had about his Order (Paragraph 27) has come abundantly true: it has flourished. But there have been controversies both internal and external which he also foresaw. Even in his own lifetime there was trouble: as early as Brother Elias there were those who could not stomach Francis' stern asceticism and found the ideal of utter poverty impracticable. And as soon after his death as 1317/18 Pope John XXII decided to go against the founder's wishes and permit his Order corporate ownership. If saints' bones turn in their graves then those of Francis must be worn smooth with revolution. Inevitably, once he himself was dead, his mantle was taken on by spirits of another sort. (Who, after all, could hope to match his charisma or the diversity of his gifts?) But the Order has survived: it has survived internal schism and attempts at reform; it has survived disputes with the Dominicans, and the attacks of Wycliffe; it has survived the French Revolution, revolutions in Spain and Poland and Italy, and in Prussia Bismarck's determined efforts at suppression.

What is the secret of Francis' unique appeal? Today we might describe it as his humanity, his warm and practical love of people and everything around him, and his witness that all stems from responding to the overwhelming love of God. His Order has given a galaxy of saints to the Church, and produced such luminaries as Clare, Bonaventure, Bernadino of Siena, Anthony of Padua, Duns Scotus, and William of Ockham. Francis is the patron saint of Italy. In 1970 Pope John Paul II proclaimed him, appropriately enough, patron saint of ecologists, and significantly it was to Assisi in 1986 that he called world religious leaders of many faiths to pray for peace.

Francis is perhaps the best loved saint of all time.

SELECT BIBLIOGRAPHY

One volume which has proved indispensable to me in my work on this translation has been the magisterial *Omnibus of Sources for the Life of St Francis*, edited by Marion A. Habig (Franciscan Herald Press 1973, co-published by SPCK in 1979). The introductions, notes and concordances are a joy to possess, and I gratefully acknowledge the extent of my debt to the *Omnibus of Sources* in general, and in particular to the contribution of Placid Hermann, OFM, who translated the *First Life* of Thomas of Celano and supplied a scholarly introduction and notes.

Other books which I have found useful in my researches are:

Adams, M., *Umbria*. Faber & Faber 1964.

Cameron, Mary Lovett, *The Inquiring Pilgrim's Guide to Assisi*. Methuen 1926.

Cuthbert Fr OSFC, *Life of St Francis of Assisi*. Longmans, Green & Co. 1914.

Della Porta P. M., Genovesi E. and Lunghi E., *Assisi: History and Art*. editrice Minerva, Assisi 1992.

Ghilardi, Agostino, 'The Life and Times of St Francis of Assisi', in *Portraits of Greatness*. Paul Hamlyn revised edn 1969.

Holland-Smith, John, *Francis of Assisi*. Sidgwick & Jackson, London 1972.

Joergensen, J., Italian translation: *San Francesco d'Assisi*, ed. Porziuncula 1983.

Von Matt, L. and Hauser, W., *St Francis of Assisi, a Pictorial Biography*. Longmans, Green & Co. 1955.

Moorman, J., *A History of the Franciscan Order from its Origins to the Year 1517*. Oxford 1968.

Sabatier, P., *Life of St Francis of Assisi*. English translation: Hodder & Stoughton, 1894.

Schmucki, Octavian OFM.Cap., *The Stigmata of St Francis of Assisi*. Franciscan Institute, St Bonaventure University, New York 1991.

Stubblebine, James H., *Assisi and the Rise of Vernacular Art*. Harper & Row 1985.

TRANSLATOR'S NOTE

My brief was to be accessible, but while some thirteenth-century Latin suggests itself readily in recognizable modern English, plenty of what Celano writes does not. The result is that my translation, like every other translation, is a compromise.

Italian names have been put into English where possible: Francesco is therefore Francis, Santa Maria della Portiuncula is St Mary of the Portiuncula, San Damiano is St Damian, and so on.

In an effort to maintain the flow of the narrative, here and there I have reduced the author's sermonizing, his effusively pious ejaculations, or fanciful allegory. In one or two cases these cuts are longer than a few lines, and I have signified them, in the usual manner, by an ellipsis. I have also generally attempted to reduce what today would be considered over-fulsome honorifics: so 'the renowned lord pope Gregory' is shortened to 'Pope Gregory'; 'most holy Poverty' becomes 'Poverty'; 'the glorious Saint Francis', or 'blessed and venerable father Francis' usually appears merely as 'Francis'.

One characteristic feature of Celano's style, which is typical of much medieval writing, is an elaborate use of repetition. Celano can be extremely laconic when it suits his purpose, so when he strives to achieve a weighty and impressive and almost incantatory effect through repetition, it would be a mistake to pare it down too ruthlessly. It would be to do violence to the author's Latin style, to lose the feeling of the original, and to betray his intentions. So in general I have let the repetition stand, and the reader must assume that it reproduces the original.

Some of the many problems facing a translator of the *First Life* can be seen if we take as an example the ending of Paragraph 121, a purple patch which displays perfectly the characteristic virtues and excesses of Thomas of Celano when he is in full flow. A close translation of this passage might be:

> The Roman pontiff, highest of all pontiffs, the leader of Christendom, the lord of the world, the shepherd of the Church, the Anointed of the Lord, the Vicar of Christ, heard all this and understood it. He was glad, he was overjoyed, he was exultant, he danced with glee when he saw the revival of God's Church in his own day by these new mysteries that were like the miracles of old, and he was delighted that it should come about through his own son, whom he bore in his sacred womb, cherished in his bosom, suckled with the word, and nourished on the food of salvation. The other prelates of the Church also heard the news, the shepherds of the flock, the defenders of the faith, the friends of the Bridegroom who stand at the pope's side, those 'hinges' of the world, the venerable cardinals. They rejoiced for the Church, they shared the pope's joy, and they glorified the Saviour, who with supreme and ineffable wisdom, with supreme and immeasurable goodness, and with supreme and incomprehensible grace chooses the foolish and lowly things of the world in order to draw the mighty to himself. The whole world heard and applauded, and the whole of Catholic Christendom abounded with joy and overflowed with holy consolation.

A paraphrase might be:

> The pope understood the importance of this and was overjoyed, especially since this religious revival had been inspired by his own spiritual son Francis. The other dignitaries of the Church shared his happiness and glorified God, as did the whole of Christendom.

Somewhere between these two extremes, one supposes, is the acceptable, accessible modern version. One has to steer a course somewhere between a rigidly literal translation, with all its unfamiliar locutions and awkward flourishes, and a totally rewritten modern paraphrase. To be strictly literal usually results in unintelligibility: to paraphrase is to exceed the translator's brief. How far one steers away from the one and towards the other is in the end a matter of taste. It is impossible to produce the perfectly successful translation. I hope at least that readers will find this one readable and intelligible.

Where psalms are referred to in the notes, the Hebrew numbering followed by, for example, the Authorized Version is given.

My translation is based on the best modern edition of Celano's *Vita Prima*, that of the Franciscans of St Bonaventure's College, Quaracchi, which appears in *Analecta Franciscana* X (1926–41).

ACKNOWLEDGEMENTS

I am happy to record my grateful thanks to Fr Gregory Shanahan OFM, who has found time to help me with various problems of interpretation; also to Sr Gillian Clare OSC, for her advice and suggestions; and to Freda Crockford for her scrutiny of the typescript and many valuable criticisms.

CHRONOLOGICAL TABLE OF EVENTS

AD

1181   Birth of Francis in Assisi, Umbria. (Christened
        Giovanni di Pietro di Bernardone, then renamed
        Francesco by his father.)

1204   Long illness of Francis. Beginning of his conversion.

1206   Trial before the Bishop of Assisi. Francis cares for
        lepers at Gubbio. Returns to Assisi and restores
        St Damian's. His conversion now complete.

1207/8 Restores St Peter's and the Portiuncula.

1208   Francis hears the Gospel at Mass on the Feast of
        St Matthias (24 February). Changes from hermit's
        habit to that of preacher. Begins to preach. Bernard,
        Peter and Giles join him, and later three more,
        including Philip.

1209   Pope Innocent III gives oral approbation of
        the Primitive Rule. Brothers move to Portiuncula.

1212   Foundation of the Second Order under St Clare.
        Abortive mission to Syria.

1213/14 Abortive mission to Morocco.

1215   Fourth Lateran Council. Francis in Rome.

1216   Honorius III becomes pope.

1217   Chapter at Portiuncula. Division of Order into
        provinces. Cardinal Hugolino and Francis meet at
        Florence.

1219   Francis goes to Palestine and preaches before the
        sultan.

1220	Francis resigns and Peter of Catania becomes Vicar of the Order. Cardinal Hugolino appointed Protector of the Order.
1221	Peter dies and Elias succeeds him as Vicar. First Rule. Rule of Third Order orally approved by Honorius III. Francis preaching in south Italy.
1222	Francis preaches in Bologna.
1223	Francis composes Second Rule at Fonte Colombo. Discussion of Second Rule at Portiuncula Chapter (June). Formal approbation of Second Rule (November). Christmas crib at Greccio.
1224	Mission sent to England (June). In September Francis receives the stigmata at La Verna. Returns to Portiuncula. Preaching tour of Umbria and The Marches.
1225	Now almost blind, visits Clare at St Damian's. Receives various treatments without improvement.
1226	In Siena for treatment. Returns again to Portiuncula. Condition worsens. Taken to the hills during the summer heat, then to palace of Bishop of Assisi. Finally returns to Portiuncula to die.
1226	Francis dies on Sunday 4 October. Buried in St George's Church.
1227	Cardinal Hugolino becomes Pope Gregory IX.
1228	Francis canonized. Thomas of Celano writes *First Life* at command of Gregory IX.
1230	Francis' remains translated to the new basilica built in his honour.

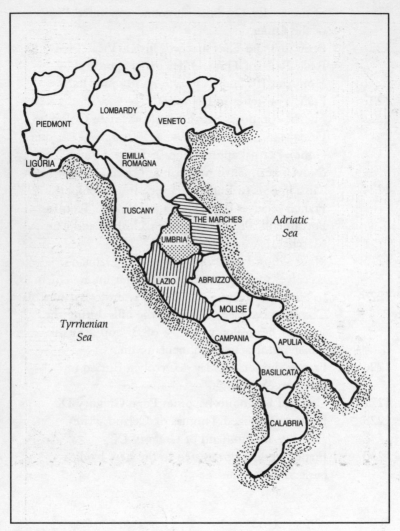

Map 1
UMBRIA in relation to the
other provinces of Italy

Map 2 (opposite)
Places of Franciscan interest

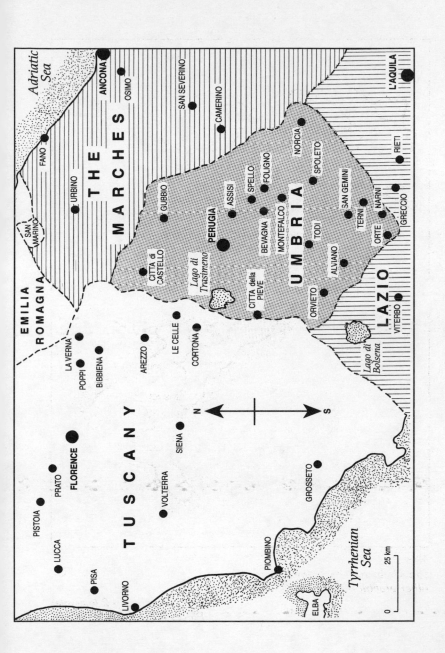

May the Grace of the Holy Spirit
be with me. In the Name of
Our Lord Jesus Christ

—

Here Begins the Prologue to
the Life of St Francis,
Founder of the Brothers Minor

1 It is my wish to write a systematic account of the life and acts of our most blessed father Francis, and to do so in humble devotion and with truth as my constant guide and teacher. But since no one can recall accurately all that he did and taught, I have endeavoured, at the request of his lordship Pope Gregory,[1] to recount to the best of my ability, however unpolished my style, all that I heard from Francis' own lips, or learnt from reliable and trustworthy witnesses. I only pray that I may deserve the name of disciple of one who always avoided verbal ambiguities and knew nothing of high-flown language.

2 I have divided all the information I could gather about the saint into three sections, subdividing the whole narrative into chapters so that the various things he did are related in order, and no doubts arise about their truth because of chronological confusion. The first part therefore keeps to the historical order of events[2] and is devoted primarily to the purity[3] of Francis' life, to his holiness of character and his teaching of the way of salvation. In this part I have included a few of the many miracles which God deigned to work through Francis while he was living in the flesh. The second part deals with the events from the penultimate year of his life up to his holy death. The third part contains many (though it omits more) of the miracles which the illustrious saint is working here on earth while reigning with Christ in heaven. It also tells of the reverence, honour, praise and glory which Pope Gregory, together with all the cardinals of the Holy Roman Church paid to Francis, when they included him in the number of saints.[4]

NOTES

1 Hugo (Hugolino or Ugolino) Conti, Count of Segni, was trained as a

lawyer and became papal chaplain, then arch-priest of St Peter's under Pope Clement III, to whom he was related. He was subsequently made cardinal-deacon by Pope Innocent III, then Cardinal-Bishop of Ostia. He became pope in AD 1227, and died in 1241. Hugo was a great champion of Francis and first Protector of the Franciscan Order.

2 In fact chronological order is not strictly adhered to.

3 'Purity' is here used in the special sense of renunciation of self and earthly things in favour of a life of complete devotion to God.

4 Francis was canonized in 1228. In fact the third part of Celano's *First Life* deals first with the canonization, secondly with the selection of Francis' miracles read out at his canonization.

PART I

To the Praise and Glory
of Almighty God,
the Father, Son and Holy Spirit.
Amen

———

Here Begins the Life of
Our Most Blessed Father Francis

Chapter I

How Francis Lived in the World
Before his Conversion

1 There was in the city of Assisi, on the borders of the valley of Spoleto,[1] a man named Francis,[2] who from his earliest years was brought up by his parents to be self-willed and to pursue the vain pleasures of the world. And having followed their wretched way of life for many years he himself became even more worldly and loose-living than they.

For this deplorable habit has taken such a strong hold on those who are called Christians, this pernicious practice is so rooted and established, as if by law, that parents do their utmost to bring up their children from the very cradle with unbelievable carelessness and laxity. No sooner do newly born children begin to speak or make their first attempts at speech, than they are taught by gestures and words of encouragement things that are utterly shameful and indecent; and when the time comes for their weaning, they are made not only to say but also to perform actions that are wholly immodest and lewd.

At this age children are naturally timid and none of them dares to behave with propriety, because if they do they are severely punished. A pagan poet[3] puts it nicely: 'We have grown up surrounded by the customs of our parents, so from our childhood every kind of evil pursues us.' This saying is true: the more parents have their way, the worse it is for the children. But then when children grow a little older and act upon their own impulses, they invariably go from bad to worse. For a diseased tree grows from a diseased root, and what is rotten through and through can rarely ever be made wholesome again. But when they have begun to embark upon their youth, what sort of persons do you imagine

7

they become? Why, they wallow in every kind of debauchery, allowed as they are to indulge their every whim; they give themselves up wholeheartedly to the service of vice. So, having become of their own volition the slaves of sin, they offer up every part of their being as an instrument of iniquity. They show nothing of the Christian religion in their lives or characters, and merely shelter behind the name of Christianity. The wretches often pretend they have committed crimes even worse than they have in fact committed, to avoid seeming the more contemptible for their comparative innocence.

2 Such were the deplorable attitudes of the society in which the man whom today we venerate as saint (for Francis is truly a saint) lived as a young man. And until almost the age of 25 he wasted and squandered his time miserably. Indeed, Francis surpassed all his friends in the worthlessness of his pursuits: he was their ringleader, always the first to suggest mischief, a zealot in the cause of folly. He was admired by everyone, and basking in empty self-glory he outdid all the others in practical jokes, in pranks, in tomfoolery, in idle talk and gossip – as he did in his dress: he wore soft, flowing garments, for he was very rich. Francis was no miser, but a wastrel: no hoarder of money, but one who spent prodigally. He was a shrewd businessman, but a hopeless manager of money. Yet for all that, he was kind in his dealings with others. He was easy-going and affable, though this was his undoing, because it was for this reason that many sought his company who were not only evildoers themselves but also egged him on to commit crimes. And so, surrounded by an army of miscreants, Francis went on his haughty and arrogant way through the highways of Babylon until the Lord looked down from heaven and for his own name's sake put his rage far from him, and checked Francis' tongue with his praise so that he might not utterly be lost. Thereafter the hand of the Lord was upon him, and a change was brought about in him by the right hand of the Most High, so that through him sinners might be assured of their restoration to

grace and his conversion to God might serve as an example to the
world.

1 Assisi is a small town in Umbria in central Italy, some ten miles east-
   south-east of Perugia, 90 miles south-east of Florence. See Map 2.
   Spoleto is also in Umbria, some 30 miles south of Assisi, and 90 miles
   north-east of Rome.
2 He was first named John (Giovanni di Pietro di Bernardone) then
   renamed Francesco, 'the Frenchman', a name uncommon at the time,
   but after his death very popular.
3 The Spanish-born Roman Seneca the Younger, c. 4 BC–AD 65. Seneca
   was a prolific writer of prose and a distinguished tragedian, but he is
   perhaps remembered chiefly today as a philosopher and orator. The
   quotation here alluded to is from a collection of essays he wrote in the
   form of letters to his friend Lucilius (*Epistulae Morales*, LX).

Chapter II
How God Visited his Heart
Through Bodily Sickness and a Vision

3 For while Francis was in the heat of youth, still ardent in sin,
  and while his lustful instincts urged him to gratify himself in
every way; and while, roused as he was by the venom of the old
serpent, he did not know how to hold himself in check, suddenly
the vengeance – or rather the grace – of Heaven came upon him,
and first tried to recall him from the error of his ways by afflicting
him with mental anguish and bodily disease, in accordance with
the prophecy of Hosea: 'Lo, I will hedge thy way with thorns and
hedge it about with a wall.'[1] So after a long and painful illness
(which is what human perversity deserves, as it can hardly ever be
corrected by anything but punishment), Francis began to reflect
upon things that had never occurred to him before.[2] Then, when
he was feeling better and, with the aid of a stick, had begun to
walk here and there around the house to speed his recovery, one

day he ventured outside and began to look upon the surrounding countryside with new eyes. But nothing he saw gave him pleasure, neither the beauty of the fields, nor the symmetry of the vineyards, nothing that normally delights the eye; and he wondered at this sudden change in himself, and began to think that people who liked such things were utter fools.

4 So from that day on he began to despise himself, and to some extent to disdain all the things he had admired and loved before – but not completely or truly, because he was not yet freed from the bondage of earthly vanity, and had not shaken from his neck the yoke of his slavery to sin. For it is very hard to give up old habits, and once things have taken root in the mind it is not easy to weaken their grip. The mind, even after a lengthy separation from them, returns to the things it was first taught, and vice, through long habituation, becomes second nature. So Francis still tried to escape the hand of God and, momentarily forgetting the lesson his Father had taught him, he basked in the smile of prosperity and thought worldly thoughts, and blind to God's plan for him made ambitious plans of his own to win empty earthly glory. For there was a certain nobleman of Assisi who was getting a sizeable military force together and, bursting with overblown ideas of self-importance, swore that he would make an expedition to Apulia[3] to win fame and fortune. When Francis heard of this, being headstrong and impulsive, he joined forces with this nobleman. He was inferior to him in point of birth, but superior in nobility of mind; his fortune was smaller, but his generosity greater.

5 Francis was wholly committed to going on this expedition, burning with desire to go, absolutely longing for the day of his departure, when one night he who had struck him with the rod of justice came to him in the sweetness of grace by means of a vision. And because Francis thirsted for glory, he beckoned him and uplifted him with a vision of the Glory of Glories. For it

10

seemed to Francis that his whole house was full of the weapons of war – saddles, shields, spears and suchlike – and this made him very happy. But then he began to ask himself what this might mean, because he had hardly been accustomed to seeing such things at home, where there were normally only bales of cloth for sale. He was puzzled, and as he wondered at this sudden turn of events, the answer came to him that all these weapons would be what he and his troops carried to war. He awoke a happy man, rose early, and taking the vision as an omen of great good fortune, he felt certain that his expedition to Apulia would go well. But he was far from the truth, and still had not the least idea of the gift heaven had bestowed on him. Yet he might have guessed that his interpretation of the vision was not the true one, because, though the vision contained some resemblance to what happened, in his heart he did not feel his former enthusiasm for such things. In fact he had to use some force on himself to press on with his plan and to undertake the journey he had set his heart on.[4]

It was indeed absolutely fitting that this vision should concern arms, and entirely appropriate that arms should be provided for a knight who was to do battle with the giant foe, so that, like a second David, he might in the name of the Lord God of Hosts free Israel from the long-standing reproach of the foe.[5]

NOTES

1 Hosea 2.6.
2 According to Celano's *Second Life* (Paragraph 4) Francis was imprisoned for a year during a civil war (AD 1202) between Assisi and Perugia, fell ill in prison and was ransomed by his father. This illness was grave and protracted, and it was during his convalescence that he underwent the change of heart that began his conversion.
3 Apulia is a province whose southernmost part forms the heel of Italy (see Map 1). It is some 200 miles south-east of Assisi. The expedition referred to here (dated 1204 or early 1205) was surely not merely for the sake of 'fame and fortune', as Celano says, but in support of papal claims in Apulia, where the Germans held sway, and was part of a larger military operation. The pope had declared that the war in the

11

south was God's holy cause, and his ally the celebrated Walter of
Brienne had been fighting there since 1202.
4 That is, Francis realized that he was not really cut out to be a soldier,
for all his dreams of glory, and if he was to go on the expedition, he
would have to force himself. (An alternative account is given by
Bonaventure, *Major Life* 1.2: after a vision, Francis goes to join the
muster at Spoleto, but when he reaches Foligno, God tells him to
return home.)
5 Compare 1 Samuel 17.26.

Chapter III

How, Having Undergone a Change of Heart, But Not Yet Wholly Converted, Francis Began to Speak Allegorically of the 'Treasure' He Had Found and His 'Bride'

---

6 Having undergone this change of heart, though not yet wholly
converted, Francis now refused to go to Apulia, and tried to
incline his will towards the will of God. So for a while he withdrew
from the hustle and bustle of the world and strove to establish
Jesus Christ in his inmost being. Like a shrewd businessman he
hid the pearl he had discovered from the eyes of the deluded, and
in secret he tried to sell all his possessions in order to buy it.[1]

Now there was a man in the city of Assisi whom Francis loved
more than any other, and since they were of the same age and their
constant association and ties of mutual affection emboldened Francis
to share his secrets with him, he would often take this friend off
to secluded spots where they could discuss private matters and tell
him that he had chanced upon a great and precious treasure. His
friend was delighted and, intrigued by what he had heard, he
gladly accompanied Francis whenever he was asked.

There was a cave near Assisi where the two friends often went
to talk about this treasure. The saint (for Francis was already a saint
by virtue of his saintly intention) would enter the cave while his

companion waited outside; and filled with a strange, new spirit he would pray to his Father in secret.

He was anxious that no one should learn what he was doing inside the cave, and finding there an opportunity for good while wisely concealing what was even better,[2] he consulted God alone concerning his secret intention. His earnest prayer was that the eternal and true God should guide his footsteps and teach him to do his will. He suffered great mental anguish, and could not rest until he had put into action what he had conceived in his heart. A variety of thoughts occurred to him one after another; they gave him no peace and disturbed him relentlessly. But he glowed inwardly with the divine fire, and was unable to conceal his spiritual ardour from others. He reproached himself for having sinned so grievously, and having offended against the sight of God's majesty; and his past sins and his present misery tormented him alike. Nor was he yet absolutely confident that he could refrain from sin in the future. So when he left the cave and rejoined his friend, he was always so exhausted with this internal struggle that he seemed a quite different person from the man who had gone in.

7 But one day after he had invoked the Lord's mercy with all his heart and soul, he was shown by the Lord what he must do. Thereafter he was filled with such elation that he was unable to contain himself, and though he did not mean to do so, he let out part of his secret in the hearing of other men. However, though he could not stay silent for the greatness of the love that inspired him, he still spoke guardedly and in veiled terms. For, while he spoke to his special friend of his 'hidden treasure', as has been mentioned, he was careful to speak to others metaphorically. He said he no longer wanted to go to Apulia, but promised to do great and noble deeds in his native country. People thought he meant to get married and asked: 'Are you thinking of taking a wife, Francis?' And he would answer them: 'I shall marry a nobler and lovelier bride than you have ever seen, one who surpasses all others in beauty and excels them all in wisdom.'

And indeed, the spotless bride of God is the true religion that Francis embraced, and the buried treasure is the kingdom of heaven that he desired with such ardour. It was absolutely necessary that the calling of the gospel should be fulfilled in one who was to be a minister of the gospel in faith and in truth.

NOTES

1 Compare Matthew 13.44: 'The kingdom of heaven is like unto treasure hid in a field; the which when a man hath found, he hideth, and for joy thereof goeth and selleth all that he hath, and buyeth that field.'
2 That is, solitude in itself was a good thing, but it was also a chance to do something even better – namely to keep secret his communion with God.

Chapter IV

How Francis Sold All His Possessions and Despised the Money He Got for Them

8 Francis was now ready, and since the appointed time had come, strengthened by the Holy Spirit, he followed the blessed impulse of his soul and set out on the road which, after worldly things have been trampled underfoot, leads on to the highest blessings. And he could delay no longer, for a fatal disease had now spread everywhere and taken such a hold on the bodies of so many people that had the physician delayed even a little while it would strangle the life out of them. So Francis armed himself with the sign of the holy cross and made a start: he saddled a horse, mounted it, and taking some scarlet cloth to sell, went in haste to the city called Foligno.[1] There, as usual, he happily sold everything he had brought and even took a sum of money for the horse he was riding and left that behind. Having disposed of all his burdens, he turned back and began to wonder in all conscience what he should do with the money he had made. In no time he was wholly engrossed in God's work – the change was miraculous – and feeling that carrying around the money even

14

for a single hour would be too much to bear, and considering that any advantage he might get from it would be like so much sand, he decided to get rid of it as soon as possible.

On his return, as he approached Assisi, he discovered near the roadside a church which had been built long ago in honour of St Damian,[2] but which threatened to collapse any moment because it was so old.

9 When Christ's new champion came abreast of this building and saw the terrible state it was in, he was moved to compassion, and with reverential awe he stepped inside. There he found a poor priest and with great respect kissed his sacred hands, offered him the money he was carrying, and told him exactly what he was planning to do. The priest was amazed. Francis' conversion seemed to him too sudden to be credible, and he refused to believe what he heard. He thought himself the victim of a hoax, and told Francis he would not accept the money he was offering him. After all, it seemed only yesterday that he had seen Francis living a dissolute life among his family and friends, and indeed behaving even more foolishly than the rest. But Francis persisted obstinately: he tried everything he could to make the priest believe him, begging him on bended knee, and entreating him to let him stay there with him for the Lord's sake. Finally the priest did let him stay, but he would not take the money because he feared what Francis' parents might do.

So Francis, who sincerely despised money, tossed it onto a window ledge, showing that he thought it no better than dust. For what he longed to possess was wisdom, which is better than gold; and to get prudence, which is more precious than silver.

NOTES

1 Foligno is a town some ten miles south-east of Assisi on the road to Spoleto.
2 St Damian's (San Damiano) is about half a mile south of Assisi.

———

15

Chapter V

How His Father Pursued Him and
Put Him in Chains

10 So while Francis was staying in the old church his father[1] went about everywhere with his eyes peeled trying to find out what had become of his son. And when he discovered what sort of life he was leading and where, he was grief-stricken and utterly furious at this sudden turn of events. He got his friends and neighbours together and went as fast as he could to St Damian's. But Francis heard of the threats of his pursuers and, learning in advance of their approach and wishing to leave their punishment to Heaven,[2] he disappeared into a hole in the ground – a secret hiding place he had made for himself for just such an eventuality. This hole was inside the priest's house and, as it happened, known to only one other person. Francis stayed there a whole month, and during that time he scarcely dared to emerge even to answer the call of nature. When food was given to him he ate it down in the hole unseen, and anything that was done for him had to be done in secret. Day and night, his cheeks running with tears, he prayed that God would deliver him from those who were persecuting him and graciously answer his prayers; fasting and weeping he entreated the Saviour's clemency, and despairing of anything he might achieve by his own effort, he cast all his burdens at the Lord's feet. And though he was confined in a dark hole in the ground, he was filled with an indescribable joy such as he had never known before; and glowing with this joy, he left his hiding place and exposed himself openly to the curses of his persecutors.

11 From that moment Francis was ardent, decisive and eager for action. Carrying before him the shield of faith to do battle for the Lord, and armed with an invincible confidence, he set out for the city and, aglow with spiritual fervour, began to accuse himself bitterly of lukewarmness and cowardice.

When all those who knew Francis saw him and thought of what he had been and what he was now, they called him every bad name they could think of. They shouted at him, denounced him as a madman, a lunatic, and threw mud and stones at him. They saw how changed he was from his earlier ways, how worn and emaciated he had become, and put it all down to madness brought on by lack of nourishment. But because patience is better than arrogance, Francis turned a deaf ear to all this: he was neither broken nor changed at all by any of the injuries he received and gave thanks to God for everything. For in vain does the evil man persecute one whose goal is righteousness: the more bruised he is, the greater his triumph will be. As someone has put it: persecution tempers a noble spirit.

12 When all this hue and cry about Francis had been going on for some time in the piazzas and streets of Assisi, and the city was echoing to the cries of people jeering at him, among the many who came to hear of it was his father. When it finally reached his ears and he heard his son's name mentioned and learned of the treatment his fellow citizens were meting out to him, he set out at once, not to rescue his son, but to ruin him. Abandoning all moderation he charged at Francis like a wolf at the fold, and with a cruel and bloodthirsty glint in his eye grabbed him, pushed him about in the most degrading fashion and dragged him back home like a criminal. There he showed him not the slightest mercy: he shut him up for days on end in a dark closet, and thinking to break his son's spirit and bend him to his will, he tried to persuade him first by argument, then by tying him up and beating him. But the only result of this was to make Francis stronger and more ready to carry out his sacred purpose: patiently he bore all the insults and his confinement in chains and never wavered for a moment. For one who is taught to rejoice in adversity cannot be turned from his just intent or made to yield in his attitude, or be plucked from Christ's flock however long he is bound and beaten. Nor does he tremble as oceans of water

break over him, when his refuge in trouble is the Son of God who, to keep us from thinking our own trials too hard to bear, always showed that those he bore were greater.

NOTES

1 Francis' father was Pietro Bernardone, a comfortably off cloth merchant; his mother Giovanna may possibly have been French.
2 The Latin says merely: 'give place to anger'. 'Anger' in the New Testament (Greek *orge* = Latin *ira*) is almost always used of divine retribution. Compare Romans 12.19.

Chapter VI

How His Mother Set Him Free, and How He Stripped Himself Naked Before the Bishop of Assisi

13 Now when Francis' father had to leave home for a while to attend to his business, Francis was left in close confinement in the house, and his mother, who had been left at home on her own with him and disapproved of what her husband had done, broke the silence and spoke to Francis. She saw that she could not dissuade him from his purpose, but moved with a mother's compassion she undid his chains and let him go free. Francis gave thanks to God and went straight back to his old lodging at St Damian's. Now that he had been tried and proved in the face of temptation, Francis allowed himself greater freedom, and after all the trials he had been through he now wore a more cheerful expression on his face. All the wrongs he had endured had given him a greater confidence, and he now went about quite freely everywhere with greater courage than previously. Meanwhile his father came back, and when he found Francis gone he made matters worse by turning on his wife and blaming her. He then rushed off, ranting and raving, to St Damian's, resolved if he failed to talk Francis into returning, at least to run him out of the province.

But to fear the Lord is to trust in his strength, and when Francis heard that his worldly father was on his way he happily and confidently went to meet him of his own free will, and told him quite frankly that being chained up and beaten meant nothing to him. He added that for Christ's sake he would gladly undergo any punishment he could devise.

14 His father saw he would never be able to deter Francis from the course he meant to pursue, and now concentrated all his efforts on recovering the money he had lost. Francis had wanted to give it all away for the feeding of the poor and for rebuilding the church. But since he had no love for money at all, he had no illusions about any good it might seem to do; and since he had no affection for it, he was quite untroubled at losing it.

When the money was found where Francis had thrown it into the dust of the window ledge, his father's rage abated a little and his mercenary instincts were somewhat pacified. He then took Francis before the Bishop of Assisi[1] and demanded that he renounce all his possessions before the prelate and give up everything he had. This Francis agreed to do, and not only that, but he happily and readily offered to do what his father demanded.

15 When Francis was brought before the bishop he could not bear to wait a moment longer. At once, before a single word was spoken, he took off his clothes, threw them all to the ground and gave them back to his father. He removed even his undergarment. He stripped himself stark naked in front of everyone. And the bishop, seeing how passionately he felt, and deeply moved by his fervour and determination, rose at once from his seat, gathered Francis in his arms and covered him with the mantle he himself was wearing. He saw quite clearly that God's hand was in this, and that what Francis had done in his presence involved a mystery. And from that moment on the bishop did all he could to help Francis; he protected him and supported him and entertained the tenderest affection for him.

St Francis Renouncing his Worldly Goods

And now Francis wrestled naked with his naked foe,[2] and having put aside all worldly things thought only of God's righteousness. Now he strove so to despise his own life, by laying aside all care for it, that he might find peace as a poor man on his troubled way,[3] and only the veil of his flesh meanwhile should keep him from the vision of God.

NOTES

1   Guido II, Bishop of Assisi until his death in 1228.
2   St Gregory (*Homilies on the Gospels*, 32) says: 'Evil spirits possess nothing of their own in this world: we must wrestle naked with a naked foe.'
3   Seneca, *Epistulae Morales* XIV 9: 'Even along a road troubled (by robbers) the poor man can be at peace.'

Chapter VII

How He Was Caught by Robbers and Thrown Into the Snow; and How He Served the Lepers

16 Now Francis, who formerly dressed in rich scarlet, was walking about half naked, and he was singing praises to the Lord in French[1] as he passed through a wood, when robbers suddenly fell upon him. In menacing tones they asked him who he was, and the saint replied confidently and firmly: 'I am the herald of the Great King. What business is it of yours?' So they beat him, and threw him into a deep ditch full of snow. 'Lie there,' they said, 'herald of God, you clodhopper!' But Francis simply shook off the snow, and when the robbers had gone leapt out of the ditch. His heart was bursting with joy, and he began to sing praises to his Creator at the top of his voice as he passed on through the wood.

At length he reached a monastery[2] and for several days, wearing nothing but a tattered shirt, worked there in the kitchen as a dishwasher, hoping for some soup to fill his belly. But he found no sympathy there, and could not get hold of any clothes, even old ones, so he left the place (not in anger, but because he was forced to by necessity) and went to the city of Gubbio,[3] where he was given a tunic by a former friend of his.

Some time after this, when the saint's fame was spreading everywhere and his name was on everybody's lips, the prior of the monastery recalled how Francis had been treated, and realizing his error went to him and humbly begged forgiveness both for himself and his monks, for the Saviour's sake.

17 Then Francis, lover as he was of perfect humility, went to a leper colony[4] and stayed among them serving them all with the most loving care for God's sake, washing all the filth from them and even wiping the pus from their sores. As he

himself writes in his *Testament*: 'When I was living in sin, I could scarcely bear even to look at lepers: but the Lord led me among them, and I took pity on them.'[5] Indeed, as he used to say, the mere sight of lepers had at one time been so disgusting to him that in the days before he was converted, if he saw one of their homes even a couple of miles away, he had to pinch his nostrils. But then by the grace and power of the Most High he began to think holy and wholesome thoughts, and one day, while he was still wearing secular clothes, he met a leper, and possessed of a strength greater than his own he went up to him and kissed him. From that day on he began to despise himself more and more, until finally, by the Redeemer's mercy, he achieved total mastery over himself.

While he was still in the world and following the ways of the world, Francis supported other poor people, too, giving a helping hand to the needy, and showing compassion to the afflicted. One day (unusually for him, as he was extremely courteous) he remonstrated with a pauper who was begging him for alms, and was at once stricken with remorse, and began to tell himself that it was a wicked sin and a positive disgrace to deny anything that was asked in the name of so great a King. So he made a solemn vow never again to deny anything it was in his power to give to anyone, if they asked it in God's name. And this he carried out to the letter; he fulfilled his vow until he had given himself away totally to others, having become, before ever he taught it, one who practised the gospel precept: 'Give to him that asketh of thee, and from him that would borrow of thee turn not thou away.'[6]

NOTES

1 During the Middle Ages it was believed that Francis' mother came from Picardy. But a more likely explanation is that the young Giovanni learned his French from his father's business acquaintances, and that this is how he acquired the nickname *il Francesco*, 'the Frenchman'.
2 Probably the Benedictine abbey of St Verecundus to the south of Gubbio.
3 Gubbio is a town with a Roman theatre at the foot of Mt Ingino, about 20 miles north of Assisi.

4 Leprosy was a term applied to a wide variety of skin diseases, both serious and relatively trivial, contagious and non-contagious.

5 Page 67, *Omnibus of Sources*. Compare Bonaventure, *Legenda Major* II.6. The quotation continues: 'When I had once become acquainted with them, what had previously nauseated me became a source of spiritual and physical consolation for me.'

6 Matthew 5.42.

Chapter VIII

How He Rebuilt the Church of St Damian; and the Life of the Ladies Who Lived There

18 Now the first piece of work that Francis undertook after freeing himself from the influence of his worldly father was to build a house for God. But he did not try to build a completely new church; he repaired an old one, and patched it up where it was in ruins. He did not pull up its foundations, but built over them, so reserving for Christ (though unwittingly) the prerogative which is his alone: for 'other foundation can no man lay than that is laid, which is Jesus Christ'.[1] And when he returned to the place where, as has been said, a church of St Damian had been built in ancient times, the grace of the Most High was with him, and in only a short time he had restored it with loving care.

St Damian's is the blessed and holy place where, some six years after Francis' conversion, and through his agency, that glorious community and most excellent Order of Poor Ladies and Holy Virgins came into being. The first and most precious stone of this foundation, and one stronger than all the others laid upon it, was the Lady Clare,[2] a native of the city of Assisi. For when, after the Order of the Brothers had been founded, Clare had been converted to God through St Francis' teaching, her life proved a boon to many, and an example to countless others. She was noble by birth, but nobler for her grace: a virgin in body, but most chaste in her heart; young in point of years, but ripe in spirit; she was unwavering in purpose, and most ardent in her longing for the love of God. She was endowed with great wisdom, and pre-eminent in humility. She was Clare[3] by name, but brighter still in her life, in her character brightest of all.

19 And above her there arose a noble structure of most precious pearls, 'whose praise is not of men, but of God',[4] since our thought is too limited to envisage it, our words too feeble to do it justice. The chief virtue these ladies possess, the one they practise above all others, is that of constant love for each other, and this so binds their wills into one that even if 40 or 50 of them live together, their unanimity makes them one in spirit. Secondly, in each one of them there glows the jewel of humility, which so preserves the good gifts heaven has bestowed on them that they are worthy of other virtues too. Thirdly, the lily of their virginity and chastity bathes them in such a wondrous fragrance that they forget all earthly thoughts and long to ponder only the things of heaven, and from the fragrance of that lily so deep a love of their eternal Spouse wells in their hearts that their devotion to holy affection banishes from them all the habits of their former lives. Fourthly, they are so distinguished for their calling to absolute poverty that never, or scarcely ever, do they permit themselves to satisfy even the most basic necessities of food and clothing.

20 Fifthly, they have so mastered the disciplines of abstinence and silence that it hardly troubles them at all to suppress fleshly urges and to curb their tongues. Some of them are so unused to conversation that when they have to speak they can scarce remember how to form the words properly. Sixthly, among all these virtues, they are endowed with such admirable patience that no adversity or trouble, no annoyance or injury can break their spirit or weaken their resolve. Seventhly, and finally, they have reached such heights in contemplation that from it they learn everything they must do, or not do. They are also fortunate

enough to be able to experience union with God in spiritual ecstasy as they persist night and day in praises and prayer. May the eternal God with his holy grace deign to grant to such a holy beginning an even holier end!

Let these words suffice for the present to describe these virgins dedicated to God, these devout handmaids of Christ: for their remarkable life and their glorious institutions, which they received from Pope Gregory (at that time Bishop of Ostia), require a separate work, and the leisure in which to write it.[5]

NOTES

1 1 Corinthians 3.11.
2 St Clare (Santa Chiara, 1194–1253) was born in Assisi of the noble Offreducci family. In 1212 she gave up all her possessions and joined Francis at the Portiuncula (see Chapter IX, note 3). Francis first placed her in a Benedictine convent, but subsequently established a separate community of women with Clare as abbess, a post she held until her death. This order became known as the Poor Clares.
3 A play on words: *clarus* in Latin means 'bright', or 'clear' or 'distinguished'.
4 Romans 2.29.
5 In fact there is a Life of St Clare commonly attributed to Thomas of Celano. See Introduction, page xiii.

Chapter IX

How Francis Changed his Habit and Rebuilt the Church of St Mary of the Portiuncula; and How, After Hearing the Gospel, He Renounced the World and Designed and Made the Habit Worn by the Brothers

21 Meanwhile Francis adopted a new style of habit,[1] and when he had repaired the church of St Damian left for another place on the outskirts of Assisi. There he began to rebuild a church[2] that was dilapidated and almost ruined and, once he had

started, he did not rest until he had put everything in perfect order. From there he went to another place called the Portiuncula[3] where a church to the Blessed Virgin Mother of God had been built in ancient times, but was now abandoned and had no one to care for it. When Francis saw it in its dilapidated state he was deeply distressed, for he was passionately devoted to the mother of all goodness, and he stayed there and started busily to rebuild it.

When he finished rebuilding the church it was the third year after his conversion. At that time he went about in a sort of hermit's garb, with a leather girdle about his waist, a staff in his hand, and wore sandals on his feet.

22 But one day[4] in that same church the gospel reading was the passage about the Lord sending out his disciples to preach. Francis was present, but he only half heard the reading, so as soon as Mass was over he humbly begged the priest to explain the reading to him. The priest went through it from beginning to end, and hearing that Christ's disciples were not to possess gold or silver or any money at all, nor to have any baggage, nor carry any staff as they went about, nor to wear shoes, nor have more than a single tunic; but that they were to preach the kingdom of God and repentance, Francis at once cried out in exultation: 'This is what I want. This is my goal. This is what I long to do with all my heart.'

In transports of joy, Francis hurried to carry out these commandments of salvation, and would let not another moment pass before beginning zealously to put into practice what he had heard. Immediately he took the shoes from his feet, laid aside his staff, made do with a single tunic, and in place of his leather girdle tied a piece of cord about his waist. He then made himself a tunic bearing the sign of the cross with which to repel all the deceits of the devil, and he made it of the roughest stuff, so that it might crucify the flesh with all its vices and sins. Lastly, he made it as mean and shabby as possible, so poor a garment that no one in the world could ever covet one. And he tried his utmost to carry out as zealously as possible all the other things he had heard. For Francis had not been deaf to the gospel message; commendably he committed everything he had heard to memory, and did his utmost to fulfil it to the letter.

NOTES

1 See the end of this Paragraph. For subsequent modifications see Paragraph 22, and Paragraph 39 for the everyday garb of the brothers.
2 Probably S. Pietro della Spina, about two miles south-east of Assisi.
3 The Portiuncula was a little church in the woods a couple of miles south-west of Assisi. It had belonged to the Benedictines of Monte Subasio but in Francis' time it was disused. It was at the Portiuncula that Francis first received his vocation; he subsequently made it his headquarters, and went there in 1226 to die.
4 Generally believed to be on the feast day of St Matthias, 24 February 1208.

———

Chapter X

His Preaching of the Gospel and Proclaiming of Peace: The Conversion of the First Six Brothers

———

23 Then with great spiritual fervour and inward elation Francis began to preach repentance to everyone, edifying all who heard him with his simple words and largeness of heart. His preaching was like a burning fire penetrating to the inmost being, and everyone who heard it was filled with admiration. He seemed quite different from the man he had once been, and as he gazed heavenwards he disdained to look on the earth. It was certainly a remarkable coincidence that he began his preaching on the very spot where he first learned to read as a small child and where he was also buried for the first time with great honour,[1] so that his auspicious beginnings might be crowned by an even more

auspicious end. Where he had learnt as a child, there he also taught: and where his mission began, there it ended in glory.

Whenever he preached, before expounding the word of God to his congregation, he would say: 'The Lord give you peace.' This was the greeting he always gave, most sincerely, to everyone, to men and women, to anyone he met or passed on the road. As a result, many who had hated peace and salvation alike, now, with the Lord's help, embraced peace with all their hearts, and became children of peace and yearned for eternal salvation.

24 Among them, a man of Assisi of pious and simple charac-ter was the first devoted follower of Francis.[2] The next to espouse the cause of peace was Brother Bernard,[3] who, to win the kingdom of heaven, zealously followed in the steps of the saint. Bernard had often shown hospitality to Francis, and having observed and acquainted himself with his character and way of life, and being inspired by the beauty of his holiness, conceived a fear of God which produced in him a longing for salvation. When he observed Francis praying all night long, sleeping only rarely, and praising God and his mother the glorious Virgin, he was moved to exclaim: 'Truly this man is from God.'

So Bernard sold all he had as quickly as possible and gave the money not to his parents but to the poor, and in order to lay claim to the way of perfection, fulfilled the command of the Holy Gospel: 'If thou wilt be perfect, go, sell that thou hast and give to the poor, and thou shalt have treasure in heaven; and come, follow me.'[4] This Bernard did, and he shared Francis' life and wore the same habit and was his constant companion until, after the numbers of the brothers increased, he was sent abroad at Francis' command. (And Bernard, who after his conversion sold all his possessions and gave them to the poor, became the model for many other converts.) Francis was overjoyed when Bernard was converted and joined him, because it seemed that in giving him the loyal friend and companion he so needed, the Lord must be showing his concern for him.

25 Immediately another citizen of Assisi joined him, a man whose way of life was beyond reproach, and who in a while was to complete an already holy life in even greater holiness.[5] Then not long after, Brother Giles[6] joined him: Giles was a simple, decent, God-fearing man who, after a long life of holiness, righteousness and piety, has left us all examples of perfect obedience, of physical endurance, of the solitary life, and of holy contemplation.

The number was made up to seven[7] by the addition of one more, Brother Philip, whose lips the Lord touched with the live coal of purity[8] so that the words he spoke about him were agreeable, and the things he uttered honey-sweet. Also, though he had had no teaching, he understood the Holy Scriptures and interpreted them, and so was following in the footsteps of those whom the leaders of the Jews called 'stupid' and 'unlettered'.[9]

NOTES

1 The church of St George in Assisi. In 1230 Francis' remains were removed from there to the new basilica.
2 His identity is unknown.
3 Bernard of Quintavalle, a noble and wealthy citizen of Assisi, who often helped Francis with alms, admired him, and finally joined him. He was one of the Order's first missionaries.
4 Matthew 19.21.
5 Thought to be Peter of Catania (d. 1221), a doctor of law who had studied at Bologna. He went to the east with Francis in 1219.
6 Giles (Brother Egidio) was received in 1208. There is an extant Life of Giles supposedly written by Brother Leo, the companion of Francis.
7 That is, counting Francis himself. Brother Philip is Philip the Long, zealous Director and Visitor of the Poor Clares.
8 See Isaiah 6.6f. Celano says: 'with the pebble [*calculo*] of purity'.
9 The apostles. See for example Acts 4.13.

29

Chapter XI

Francis' Gift of Prophecy and
the Admonitions He Gave

26 Each day Francis was filled with the comfort and grace of the Holy Spirit as, with the utmost vigilance and care, he instructed his new sons in their new way of life, teaching them to walk with unwavering steps the way of holy poverty and blessed simplicity.

One day as he was contemplating the Lord's great mercy in the blessings he had showered upon him, and longing for the Lord to reveal what the future might hold for him and his Brothers, he went to his place of prayer, as he had done so often. There he persisted in prayer for a long time, waiting on the Ruler of the Universe with fear and trembling, and reflecting bitterly upon all the years he had wasted; and he kept repeating the same words: 'God, be merciful to me, a sinner', until gradually an indescribable joy and overpowering sweetness began to flood into the core of his being. He fell into a trance of ecstasy, and suddenly all the doubts he had entertained were silenced, all the darkness that had gathered in his heart through fear of sin was dispelled. The certainty that all his sins were forgiven poured over him, and he was granted an assurance of his restoration to grace. Then he was rapt in spirit and wholly absorbed in a halo of light; his mental powers were enhanced and he could see quite clearly what was to happen. Finally when the light faded and the rapture passed he felt spiritually reborn, and he emerged from the experience a quite different person.

27 So he returned to his Brothers and said happily:

Take heart, dear Brothers, and rejoice in the Lord. Do not be downcast because you seem so few, and do not worry about my simplicity or your own. For the Lord in his truth has shown me a vision: God will turn us into a vast multitude; he will swell our numbers until we reach the ends of the earth. I must also tell you for your own good what else I saw: I would much rather be silent about it, but charity compels me to tell you.

I have seen a great multitude of men coming to us and wishing to wear the habit of our holy Brotherhood and to live with us under our religious rule. Indeed, I can still hear the sound they make as they go and come back in answer to the call of holy obedience. I have seen the highways teeming with them as they gather here in their tens of thousands from almost every nation on earth. Frenchmen are coming, Spaniards are hurrying here, Germans and Englishmen are running to join us, and numberless hordes of others speaking every language under the sun make haste to be with us.

When the Brothers heard this they were overjoyed, both for the grace which the Lord God had bestowed on his saint, and also because they so ardently longed for the good of their fellow-men, and desired that those destined to be saved in their Brotherhood should swell their numbers daily.[1]

28 Francis also said to them:

Brothers, in order to give thanks faithfully and sincerely to our Lord God for all his gifts to us, and so that you may know what sort of life the brothers, present and to come, are to live, you must understand the truth about what is going to happen.

Now as we begin our life together we shall find fruits that are sweet and delicious to eat; but after a while we shall be offered fruits that are less delicious and sweet, and finally we shall be given some that are full of bitterness, which we shall not be able to eat because their bitterness makes them inedible, though they may smell and look good enough on the outside. Now as I have told you, the Lord will indeed increase us and make our Brotherhood great. But in the end the same will happen as when a man casts his nets into the sea or a lake and catches a great haul of fish. When he has got them into his boat, he cannot be bothered to take them all ashore because they are so many. So he picks out the biggest and best and those he likes the look of, and puts them in his baskets, and the rest he throws overboard.

The obvious truth of all these predictions Francis made is clear enough to anyone who considers them impartially, and their subsequent fulfilment offers irrefutable proof of his prophetic gifts.

NOTE

1 A clear echo of Acts 2.47: 'And the Lord added to the church daily such as should be saved.'

Chapter XII

How He Sent the Brothers Two by Two Throughout the World, and How Shortly Afterwards They Were Gathered Together Again

29 At the same time too another good man joined the Brotherhood and increased their number to eight.[1] Francis then called them all together and spoke at length about the kingdom of God, the rejection of the world, the renunciation of their own will, and the subjugation of their bodies. He then split them into four groups of two and said to them:

Go, my dearest brothers, two by two through your different parts of the world, proclaiming peace to mankind and repentance for the remission of sins. And be patient in affliction, confident that the Lord will fulfil his purpose and make good his promise. When men question you, reply with humility; bless those who persecute you, give thanks to those who wrong you and slander you, because it is these things that win us a place in the eternal kingdom.

Overjoyed, the Brothers accepted the command of holy obedience and humbly prostrated themselves on the ground before Francis. He embraced them with sincere affection and said to each of them: 'Cast your care upon the Lord and he will sustain you'.[2] These were the words he always spoke when he sent any of the Brothers off on a mission.

30 Brother Bernard then set off with Brother Giles to Santiago de Compostela.[3] Francis himself with his companion chose a different part of the world; and the remaining four, travelling in pairs, covered the regions that were left. But after only a short time Francis longed to see them all again, so he prayed to the Lord (who gathers the scattered tribes of Israel) of his mercy to deign to bring them together again soon. And so it happened that shortly after, just as Francis had desired, and answering no human summons, the brothers came together again, all giving thanks to God as one. And when they met, they were overjoyed to see their faithful shepherd, and amazed that they had all decided to return again at the same time. They then reported all the favours the Lord had granted them, and if they proved to have been in any way negligent or ungrateful they humbly begged the holy father's correction and discipline, and obeyed it to the letter. For this had always been their custom when they came to Francis, and they never concealed from him the slightest thought or even the momentary impulses of their hearts. And even when they had carried out all they had been commanded to do, they considered themselves worthless servants.[4] For those first disciples of Francis were so imbued with the spirit of purity that though they knew they were doing useful and holy and righteous things, it would never have occurred to them to congratulate themselves.

31 Francis embraced his sons with the deepest affection and began to reveal his intentions to them and to tell them what the Lord had revealed to him. And at once four other men, all of them good and sincere, were added to their number and followed the saint.[5] There was great talk of this among the people and Francis' reputation began to spread further afield. Indeed at that time Francis and his brothers were jubilant whenever any faithful layman was led by the spirit of God to come and receive the religious habit; their joy was unconfined, whoever he was and

of whatever condition – rich or poor, noble or lowborn, loathed or loved, wise or simple, literate or illiterate.

All these things excited the admiration of the outside world too, and the example of humility inspired people to mend their ways and repent of their sins. No disadvantage, neither low birth nor poverty, could stand between Francis and the nurture of those God had chosen for him; for God delights to be with the outcasts of the world and with the simple.

NOTES

1 See Chapter X, note 7. The name of this new brother is not known.
2 Psalm 55.22 in the wording of the Roman Psalter, the version used in all churches in Italy up to the time of Pius V (1566–72): 'Cast thy care upon the Lord and he shall sustain thee.' The more familiar AV has 'Cast thy burden', etc.
3 The shrine in Galicia in the north-west of Spain where St James the Apostle is said to be buried, a centre for pilgrimages from all over the world, and in the Middle Ages second only to Jerusalem in importance.
4 See Luke 17.10: 'So likewise ye, when ye shall have done all those things which are commanded you, say: We are unprofitable servants: we have done that which was our duty to do.'
5 This brought the total to 12, including St Francis himself. These first 12 Brothers are thought to be: Francis, Bernard of Quintavalle, Peter of Catania, Giles, Sabbatino, Morico, John of Capella, Philip the Long, John of St Constantia (San Constanzo), Barbaro, Bernard Viridante, and Angelo Tancredi.

<hr>

Chapter XIII

How, When He Had 11 Brothers, He Wrote His First Rule; and How Pope Innocent III Confirmed It; His Vision of the Tree

32 Seeing that the Lord God was daily increasing the number of his followers, Francis composed a permanent guide and a rule of life for himself and his Brothers.[1] He wrote it in simple,

concise language, using chiefly the words of the Holy Gospel, for it was the perfection of the gospel alone he yearned for. But he also added a few other things that were essential for the practice of a holy life. Then with all of his brothers he went to Rome hoping and praying that Pope Innocent III[2] would confirm the rule he had written. Now Guido,[3] the venerable Bishop of Assisi, was at Rome at that time, and he admired Francis and his brothers in all they did, and felt a special affection for them. When he saw Francis and his brothers, he did not know why they had come, and was perturbed, because he feared that they might wish to leave their native country where the Lord had already begun to achieve so much through them. He was overjoyed to have men of such holiness in his diocese and believed that wonders might be achieved by their saintly life and example. But when he heard why they had come, and realized what they wanted, he gave joyful thanks to God and promised to give them his advice and to help

Pope Innocent III Approving the Rule

35

them to achieve their purpose. Francis also went to visit the Bishop of Sabina, John of St Paul,[4] who more than any of the princes and dignitaries of the Roman Curia seemed to despise worldly things and to love the things of heaven. Bishop John received Francis kindly and affectionately, and expressed warm approval of what he proposed to do.

33 But, being a far-sighted and shrewd man, he proceeded to question Francis on a number of points, and tried to persuade him to become a monk or a hermit.[5] Francis, as humbly as he could, resisted his persuasion, not out of any disrespect for the bishop's advice, but because in his devout longing for a different way of life he was inspired by a loftier desire. The bishop was profoundly moved by his fervour but, thinking that the life he proposed would be too severe, suggested to him paths that would be less arduous. But finally he was won over by Francis' persistence and gave way to his entreaties, and subsequently did all he could to advance his cause with the pope. At that time the head of the Church was Pope Innocent III, an illustrious prelate and a man of vast learning, renowned for his preaching and for his zealous promotion of all that the practice of the Christian faith demanded. When the pope learnt what Francis and his brothers were asking, after due consideration he granted their petition[6] and carried it into complete effect. Then, after offering them his encouragement and giving his advice on a great many matters, he blessed Francis and his brothers and said:

> Go with the Lord, Brothers, and, as the Lord sees fit to inspire you, preach repentance to all men. When Almighty God increases you in number and in grace, come back to me with joy, and I will grant you further privileges and give you greater powers with more confidence.

Truly the Lord was with Francis wherever he went, gladdening him with visions and cheering him with blessings at every turn. One night, for example, when he had fallen asleep, it seemed to him that he was walking along a road and at the side of this road there was a very tall tree. It was a beautiful, sturdy tree with a thick trunk and it towered on high. As Francis walked over to it and admired its beauty and majestic height, he suddenly became so tall himself that he could touch the top of the tree, and he took hold of it, and effortlessly bent it to the ground. And indeed this is what happened, because Pope Innocent, the loftiest and most exalted tree in the world, inclined his ear to Francis' petition and graciously bowed to his will.

NOTES

1 The first, or 'primitive' Rule, which is no longer extant.
2 Innocent III, pope from 1198 to 1216, had studied theology at Paris and canon law at Bologna. Under him the Roman See enjoyed the greatest power and prestige in its entire history, and he is regarded as the greatest of all the medieval popes. During his pontificate both the Franciscan and Dominican Orders came into being, and it was he who convoked the Fourth Lateran Council of 1215 (in which the doctrine of the Eucharist was defined). Innocent III is also celebrated for the determined stand he took against heretics, especially the Albigensians.
3 See Chapter VI, note 1 above. This is the bishop before whom Francis stripped naked, renouncing all his worldly possessions.
4 Giovanni di San Paolo, a Benedictine who had studied medicine at Salerno. He was made Cardinal-Bishop of Santa Sabina in 1204 and was Francis' first official contact with the Roman hierarchy. He died in 1215.
5 That is, to join some existing Order.
6 This was oral approbation only, provisional and qualified (granted probably in April 1209): Innocent III, who was desperate to keep the Church unified and to resist the threat of breakaway movements, clearly had reservations about a new, unorthodox order aiming at absolute perfection and living wholly without property. No doubt the austerities of Francis' rule seemed to him to smack of the perfectionism of his arch-enemies the Catharists. However, he saw something genuine in Francis and his followers, so he was prepared to give them his qualified backing. This verbal approbation did not make Francis' Brothers clerics, but it did give them a certain official standing as evangelizers, and subsequently Innocent's verbal approval was regarded as constituting the Brotherhood an Order.

Chapter XIV

His Return from Rome to the Valley of Spoleto
and the Stop He Made Along the Way

━━━

34 Francis and his brothers were jubilant at the gracious gift of the pope and gave thanks to Almighty God, who exalts the humble and comforts all who sorrow. He at once went to visit the shrine of St Peter and, after saying his prayers there, left the city and set out with his companions towards the valley of Spoleto.

On this journey they talked together about all the great blessings God in his infinite mercy had bestowed upon them, and their warm reception by the Vicar of Christ, the lord and father of all Christendom; they discussed how they could best act upon his advice and fulfil his commands, how they could sincerely observe the rule they had taken upon themselves, and keep it faithfully; how they might walk in all faith and holiness before the Most High; and finally how, as they progressed in the Christian virtues, their life and conduct might be an example to their neighbours.

At length, when Christ's new disciples had sufficiently discussed all these matters with due humility, time had flown and the day was almost gone. By now they had come to a desolate spot; they were tired from their journey and hungry, but could find nothing to eat anywhere because the place was so remote and there were no houses nearby. But at once, in his mercy, God saw to their needs: a man came up to them with a loaf of bread in his hand, gave it to them and went away again. The Brothers were amazed, as they did not know this man; and each encouraged his neighbour to have greater confidence in God's mercy. When they had eaten they felt much better, and they travelled on to a place near the city of Orte,[1] where they spent about a fortnight. Some of them went into the city to get the supplies they needed, and brought back to the others what little they had been able to get by begging from door to door: and this they all ate together with thankful and joyful hearts. If anything was left over, and if they could find no one to give it to, they would hide it in an abandoned tomb where the bodies of the dead had once lain, so they could have it to eat another time. This place where they were staying was desolate and remote, and no one, or very few people, ever went there.

35 But the Brothers were at their happiest when they could neither see nor possess anything which might give them vain or worldly pleasure. So it was there that they first communed with holy poverty; and greatly comforted by the lack of all worldly things, they decided to cling to poverty everywhere, just as they were doing here. And because they had cast aside all worldly cares, and delighted only in the comfort of heaven, they firmly resolved never to shrink from its embraces, whatever troubles assailed them, whatever temptations beset them. Though they found the place most agreeable (a fact which can easily undermine even the strongest of wills) they did not allow themselves to become too attached to it, and in case a longer stay might seem to imply some degree of ownership, they left, and following Francis went next to the valley of Spoleto. And since they sincerely longed for righteousness, they discussed among themselves whether they should live among men or take themselves off to somewhere solitary. But Francis, who trusted not in any virtue of his own, but prefaced all such business with prayer, chose not to live for himself alone, but for him who died for us all, knowing that it was his mission to win for God the souls that the devil was trying to make off with.

NOTE

1 Orte is on the right bank of the Tiber some 40 miles north of Rome, to the west of Viterbo.

━━━━

Chapter XV

Francis' Fame; the Conversion of Many to God; How the Order Was Called the Order of Friars Minor; Francis' Instruction of Those Who Entered the Order

36 Then Francis, the valiant champion of Christ, went round the cities and hill towns proclaiming the kingdom of God, preaching peace, teaching salvation and repentance for the forgiveness of sins; and this he did, not by persuading people with words of human wisdom, but with the knowledge and the power of the Spirit. In all he did he had complete confidence, a confidence he drew from the authority the pope had conferred on him; he used no cajoling words or flattery to win over his listeners. He did not know how to smoothe over people's sins, only how to pierce them through; he could not be indulgent towards the lives of sinners, he could only flay them with harsh reproof, because he had first convinced himself in practice of the things he was urging others to do in his preaching. Without fear of censure he spoke the truth, and even the most learned of men, men of rank and renown, would marvel at his preaching and benefit from being quite awestruck at his presence. Men came running, women too came running, priests and religious hurried to see and hear the saint, who seemed to them all some creature from another world. People of every age, both male and female, eagerly made their way to see these miracles which the Lord was now working in the world through his servant Francis. Indeed it seemed at that time – whether it was because of Francis' presence, or the reputation he enjoyed – that a new light had been sent to earth from heaven scattering all the gloom and darkness which had covered virtually the whole of that region, and covered it so thickly that scarcely anyone knew which way to go. For the burden of sin lay heavy on almost everyone; people showed such total disregard of God, such a careless disregard of his commandments

that they were extremely loath to be roused from even the least of their sins, which were habitual and deeply ingrained.

37 Francis gleamed like a star shining in the dimness of night, and like morning spread upon the darkness. And so it happened that in a short time the whole face of the province was changed. Everywhere the old filth of sin was removed, and it appeared a happier, more cheerful place. The former aridity of the land was banished, and crops quickly sprang up in fields that were lately neglected. The uncultivated vine began to put forth shoots of heavenly fragrance, and after sprouting blossoms of wonderful sweetness, produced fruits of honour and righteousness. Everywhere there was the sound of praise and thanksgiving, and as a result many cast away worldly cares and gained knowledge of themselves in the life and teaching of Francis, and they burned with a desire to love and revere their Creator. Many people, both noble and lowborn, both clergy and lay, were inspired by God and began to come to Francis, all eager to do battle at his side, to follow his rule and obey his command for ever. Francis, like a deep-flowing river of heavenly grace, watered them all with streams of spiritual gifts, and embellished the field of their hearts with the flowers of virtue. He was truly a master of his art, and after his example, through his rule and teaching and ringing proclamation of the gospel, the Church of Christ is being renewed with a flood of converts, and triumphing in a threefold army[1] of souls destined for salvation. To each of them he gave a rule of life, and unerringly showed them the way to salvation whatever their position in life.

38 But the main subject of this work is an account of the Order which Francis, both out of charity and by profession, founded and led. The facts are these: it was Francis himself who first founded the Order of Friars Minor and at its foundation gave it that name. For, as is well known, he wrote in the Rule: 'And let them be *lesser*'. And in the very same hour he confirmed what he

had written in the Rule by saying: 'It is my wish that this brother-hood be called the Order of Lesser Brethren.' Indeed they were 'lesser', always putting others before themselves, and seeking somewhere lowly to live and work to do which involved them in some sort of hardship, so that this should give them a solid grounding in humility, and as the other virtues were successfully set in place, a spiritual fabric of all the virtues might rise up among them. And indeed upon this enduring foundation there rose the glorious edifice of charity, built from a mass of living stones gathered from every part of the world to form a dwelling place for the Holy Spirit.

Oh, with what fervent charity these new disciples of Christ burned! What love for their holy fellowship flourished among them! For whenever they came together anywhere or met each other by chance on the road, a shoot of spiritual love sprang into being which scattered over all love the seed of true affection.

What more can I say of their virtues? Their embraces were chaste, their disposition benign, their kisses holy, their conversation agreeable, their laughter modest, their appearance genial, their gaze honest, their spirit humble, their speech conciliatory, their answer soft, their purpose single, their obedience swift and their efforts unflagging.

39 Since they despised all worldly things and their love for one another was never selfish, they were able to pour out all their affection upon the whole community, and all alike strove to give themselves in order to meet their Brothers' needs. They loved each other's company, and loved even more to live together. Whenever two Brothers parted there was mutual sadness; the leave-taking was bitter, the separation painful. But they dared put nothing before the commands of holy obedience. Before a com-mand was even uttered, these most obedient soldiers of Christ would be ready to fulfil it; treating all commands as equally binding, without a word of protest they almost fell over themselves to do whatever they were told to do. As followers of poverty they

had nothing, and loved nothing, and so had no fear of losing anything. They were content with a single tunic which was sometimes patched inside and out. It was not an elegant garment, but shabby and coarse, so that those who wore it might seem absolutely crucified to the world. They wore belts of rope and undergarments of cheap material. And it was their pious resolution to remain in this state and to have nothing more. So they were entirely secure, with nothing to fear; and with no cares to distract them they awaited each new day without the slightest anxiety; though frequently in great difficulties on their travels, they never worried about finding lodging for the night. For if, as often happened, they had nowhere to stay and it was freezing cold, they huddled together in some outhouse[2] or meekly lay down in wayside tombs or caves. During the day those who had a skill worked with their hands, and stayed in lepers' houses, or other lowly[3] places, serving everyone there with humility and devotion.

They would never engage in any activity which might give rise to scandal, but by always doing work that was holy and virtuous, decent and useful, they inspired everyone they came into contact with to emulate their own humility and patience.

40 They were so imbued with the virtue of patience that they actively sought to be in situations where they might suffer persecution, rather than where, if people came to know of their holiness and spoke well of it, worldly approbation might make them proud. For many times after being abused, insulted, stripped, beaten and tied up or thrown into prison, they called on no one to protect them, and bore everything so courageously that the only words to escape their lips were those of praise or thanksgiving. Rarely if ever did they cease from praising God or from prayer; by continuous self-examination they recalled all they had done and offered up thanks to God for what they had done well, and for what they had left undone, or done rashly, they offered up groans and tears. They thought they were forsaken by God if their customary piety deserted them for a moment in their devotions.

43

So when they wanted to concentrate on prayer, they used various devices to stop themselves falling asleep. Some held on to ropes to stay upright in case sleep stole over them and their prayer was disrupted. Some put chains of iron[4] about them, others confined themselves in girdles of wood. If ever they were guilty of intemperance – if, through tiredness after their travels they exceeded the bounds of necessity in what they ate or drank by even the tiniest amount – they would torture themselves most cruelly by fasting for days on end. In short they were so single-minded in their efforts to quell the urges of the flesh by mortification that they would often actually strip naked in the iciest weather and plunge thorns into themselves all over their bodies until they were covered in blood.

41 For they were so resolved to despise all earthly things that they were loath to allow themselves even the barest necessities of life; and so long had they been strangers to bodily comfort that no hardships could trouble them. And while they lived this life, they strove for peace and meekness in their relations with others; by always behaving in a seemly and peaceable way they made sure to avoid any possible scandal. Since they hardly spoke even when speaking was necessary, and no frivolous or idle word ever escaped their lips, there was no room for anything immodest or indecent in any part of their daily lives. Their every action was disciplined, their every movement was modest. All their bodily senses were so mortified that they scarcely allowed themselves to hear or see anything except what suited their purpose. They fastened their eyes upon the ground, but their minds were fixed upon heaven. No envy or malice, spite or slander, suspicion or bitterness found a place among them: there was instead a deep harmony, perpetual quiet, and the voice of praise and thanksgiving. These were the principles upon which Francis, like a gentle father, moulded his new sons; and he taught them not by words alone, but above all by showing the truth of what he preached in practice.

1 The three Orders founded by Francis: first, the Friars Minor; secondly the Poor Clares; and thirdly the tertiary Order for lay people.

2 The Latin word translated as 'outhouse' is *clybanus*, which means 'oven' or 'furnace'. This is surely what Italians call the *forno* – a (usually circular) outhouse, or extension of the house, where the bread is baked.

3 Text: most translations have 'decent' (*honestis*); but one manuscript has the opposite *inhonestis*, and this seems to fit the context better.

4 These grim instruments of discipline are only vaguely described and cannot be precisely identified. The chain might perhaps be a wire noose with points turning inwards which was strapped round the fleshy part of the thigh so that any sort of movement caused intense pain. Archaic as it may sound, this device was still used by Jesuit novices in the days of Gerard Manley Hopkins.

Chapter XVI

His Stay at Rivo Torto and His Observance of the Rule of Poverty

42 Francis and his Brothers then went to a place near the city of Assisi called Rivo Torto.[1] There they found an abandoned shack and the Brothers, who so despised grand and beautiful houses, lived beneath its shelter and so protected themselves from the wind and rain. (For, as another saint said,[2] it is easier to get to heaven from a hut than from a palace.) There with their saintly father all his sons and brothers lived together in conditions of great hardship and need: they were regularly deprived even of the solace of bread, and had to make do with turnips alone which in their dire straits they went begging for here and there over the plain of Assisi. The shack which sheltered them was so cramped that they could scarcely sit down, let alone sleep, in it.

But there was no murmur of resentment or complaint about any of this; since their hearts were serene, and their minds were full of joy, they remained patient. Francis was scrupulous in his examination both of himself and his Brothers, and this he did daily, in fact continuously. He allowed them not the slightest room for wantonness, and banished all negligence from their hearts. He was rigid in his discipline, and kept a strict watch over himself every hour of the day. If any normal, bodily temptation assailed him, he would throw himself into a pit (which in winter would be full of ice) and stay there until every carnal thought had left him. And indeed the others were most zealous in following his stern example of self-mortification.

43 He taught them not only to mortify vices and to curb fleshly urges, but also to subdue even the outward senses themselves, through which death enters the soul. When the Emperor Otto[3] was passing through this part of Italy, with much pomp and ceremony, to receive the crown of the Holy Roman Empire, Francis was living with his Brothers in the shack described above near the road along which Otto was travelling; and he neither left it to see the procession, nor allowed anyone else to look except for one of the Brothers who was to call out repeatedly to the emperor that this glory of his would last only a short time.[4] For the saintly Francis was living his own interior life, and as he grew in largeness of soul, was preparing in himself a dwelling fit for God. So no worldly din claimed his attention, no sound of any sort could disturb or interrupt the lofty business upon which he was engaged. The authority conferred on him by the pope gave him great confidence, and for that reason he utterly refused to flatter kings or princes.

44 He devoted himself at all times to holy simplicity, and never allowed his meagre lodgings to cramp the greatness of his heart. He wrote the names of the Brothers on the beams of the shack so that each of them had his own place to go if he wanted to pray or to rest, and his mental tranquillity should not be disturbed by the lack of space. One day during their stay at Rivo Torto, a man leading an ass came along to the shack where Francis and his brothers were sheltering and, not wanting to be

turned away, he egged his ass on to go inside. 'In you go,' he said; 'we shall do well in this place.' Francis was deeply disturbed when he heard this, because he realized what was in the man's mind. (He obviously thought that the Brothers wanted to settle there for good and to enlarge the place by building onto it.) So out came Francis at once, and abandoned the shack because of what the peasant had said, and went off to another spot not far away called the Portiuncula where, as has been said, there was a church of St Mary, the church that he himself had rebuilt many years before. In order to possess the Lord only, and so possess everything in greater fulness, Francis wanted nothing at all in the way of property.

NOTES

1 Rivo Torto is a mile or so south of the Portiuncula on the road to Spello.
2 The saint's name is not known.
3 Emperor Otto IV of Brunswick was crowned emperor by Innocent III on 4 October 1209. It is not known whether he passed by Rivo Torto en route for, or on his return from, Rome.
4 Otto was excommunicated in 1210 for failing to protect the rights of the Church. Frederick II was crowned in his place in 1212. Otto was decisively defeated at the Battle of Bouvines in 1214, and died four years later.

———

Chapter XVII

How Francis Taught his Brothers to Pray.
Their Obedience and Purity

———

45 It was then that the Brothers begged Francis to teach them to pray, for because of their simplicity of spirit they knew nothing of the offices of the Church. He said to them: 'When you pray, say "Our Father" and "We worship you, O Christ, here and in all your churches all over the world, and we bless you since by

your holy cross you have redeemed the world."' This command the Brothers, as obedient disciples of their master, were at pains to observe with the utmost care. For they endeavoured to carry out most faithfully not only the things Francis told them by way of brotherly advice, or commanded them to do as their father in God, but even the things he was thinking or meditating upon, if there was some way of finding them out. For Francis used to tell them that true obedience was not only a matter of doing what one is told by a superior, but responding to his merest thoughts; it was not just carrying out whatever he ordered, but whatever he inwardly desired. That is, when a Brother hears the command of a superior Brother and understands the thought behind that command, then he should immediately devote himself wholly to obeying him and to doing whatever he understands, by whatever token, to be his will.

Moreover, whenever they saw a church, even indeed if they were miles away and could only see it from a great distance, they would prostrate themselves on the ground towards it, showing it reverence both spiritually and physically, and would worship the Almighty with the words: 'We worship you, O Christ, here and in all your churches', as their holy father had taught them. And, what was no less remarkable, whenever they saw a cross, or something in the shape of a cross, whether on the ground or on a wall or in the branches of trees or in the hedges along the roadside, they performed the same obeisance.

46 They had become so filled with the spirit of simplicity, were being so schooled in innocence of life, so possessed by purity of heart that they knew nothing of deceitfulness. As they were united in faith, so they were united in spirit, in will, in charity; their hearts and minds were as one; their daily lives were characterized by the perfect harmony of their behaviour, their cultivation of the virtues, their complete unanimity, and the piety of their actions.

At one time the Brothers were confessing their sins to a certain secular priest who was deservedly notorious for all the wicked things he had done. But though they were told of his wickedness by many different people, they would not believe it, and so they went on confessing their sins to him as usual, and paying him the respect due to a priest. And when this priest (or it may have been some other priest) said one day to one of the Brothers, 'Beware of hypocrisy, Brother', this Brother at once believed he must be a hypocrite, because of what the priest had said, and as a result he wept day and night and was quite overcome with grief. When the Brothers asked him what was the meaning of all this moaning and groaning (which was quite unlike him), he told them: 'A priest said something to me that has caused me so much grief I can scarcely think of anything else.' The Brothers tried to comfort him and urged him not to believe it, but he said to them: 'What can you be saying, Brothers? It was a priest who said this to me. Can a priest lie? Well, since a priest cannot lie, we must believe that what he said is true.' And he persisted for some considerable time in this naive misunderstanding until finally he was comforted by Francis, who pointed out the real meaning of the priest's remark, and shrewdly explained his purpose in making it. Scarcely any of the Brothers could ever be so deeply troubled in mind that as soon as Francis spoke, his brilliant warmth did not dispel every cloud, and bring back a sky of blue.

Chapter XVIII

Of the Fiery Chariot; and Francis' Knowledge of What Was Happening Elsewhere

47 The Brothers, walking in simplicity before God and with confidence before people, were now considered worthy to be cheered by a divine revelation. One night, kindled by the fire of the Holy Spirit, they were chanting the *Pater Noster* in harmonious and suppliant tones (this they did not only at the appointed hours

but at every hour, since earthly cares and worldly anxieties affected them little) when Francis happened to leave them. And lo and behold, at about midnight, while some were sleeping and the rest were praying devoutly in silence, a dazzling chariot of fire came through the doorway and turned about this way and that two or three times inside the house. Above it rested a huge orb, like the sun, which made the night as bright as day. Those awake were stunned, those who were sleeping awoke in alarm; and they felt the light shining as brightly in their hearts as on their bodies. They gathered together and began to ask each other what was the meaning of this vision, but by the power and grace of that brilliant light they could all read what was in their neighbour's heart. And finally they knew: they realized that it was the soul of their holy father that had shone with such dazzling splendour, and that it was because of his exceptional purity and tender care for his sons that he had been found worthy to receive the blessing of this great gift from God.

48 And indeed they had the clearest proof of this, and had learned from experience that the secrets of their hearts were not hidden from their most holy father. How often, through a revelation of the Holy Spirit, Francis knew what his Brothers were doing, though they were far away, and no one had told him! How often he brought to light the secrets of their hearts, and explored their consciences! How many he appeared to in their sleep and told them what they must do, or warned them that they must not do! And how often he predicted that no good would come of Brothers whose behaviour at the time appeared good! In the same way, too, he would know in advance if certain Brothers were to overcome their sins, and could assure them that they would win the grace of salvation. What is more, if any Brother deserved to be rewarded for his purity and simplicity, he was granted the special consolation of seeing the saint in a way the rest had never experienced. I will give just one example of this, a story related to me by reliable witnesses.

Once when Brother John of Florence[1] was appointed by Francis as minister of the community in Provence and he had been holding a chapter of the Brothers there, the Lord God in his unfailing mercy inspired him with eloquence and made all the Brothers attentive and eager to hear him. Among the Brothers there was one called Monaldo, a priest of great repute, whose holiness of life was even greater. His virtue was founded on humility, sustained by frequent prayer, and preserved by the shield of patience. Brother Anthony[2] was also present at this chapter, and the Lord enlightened his mind so that he could understand the Scriptures and utter words about Jesus before everyone present that were 'sweeter than honey and the honeycomb'.[3] While Anthony was preaching a sermon of fiery intensity on the text 'Jesus of Nazareth, King of the Jews', this Brother Monaldo glanced towards the door of the house where they were all gathered and there, with his bodily eyes, he saw Francis high above the ground with hands outstretched, as if he were on a cross, blessing the Brothers. Everyone there seemed to be filled with the comfort of the Holy Spirit, and the great spiritual joy they experienced led them to believe unhesitatingly what Monaldo told them about his vision and the presence of Francis among them.

49 There are many stories of people having experience of the saint's ability to know the secrets of other men's hearts. I will relate just one, about which there can be no possible doubt.

A brother named Riccerio,[4] a nobleman by birth, but one nobler still by nature, a man who loved God and despised himself, was led by the eager desire of a godly heart to win and to enjoy forever the favour of the holy father Francis, but he was seriously worried that Francis might have some private reservation about him and keep him at arm's length. Being a God-fearing man he thought that whomever Francis loved deeply would also be worthy of God's favour, but conversely anyone to whom Francis was not well disposed or favourably inclined would incur the wrath of the Judge on High. These were the thoughts Riccerio was turning over in his mind; these were the things he kept saying to himself in private, though he told nobody about it.

50 But one day, when Francis was in his cell praying, Riccerio came by, troubled with his usual thoughts, and the saint both knew of his arrival and sensed what he was worried about. He at once sent for him and said:

> Do not be disturbed, my son, and do not let your thoughts disturb you, for you are very dear to me. I assure you, you are indeed worthy of my love and friendship, and a place among those I hold especially dear. Feel free to visit me whenever you wish, and speak to me with confidence, as friend to friend.

Riccerio was dumbfounded, and thereafter he became even more reverent, and as he grew in the saint's affection, so he learned to have greater trust in God's mercy.

How hard your absence is, holy father, for those who have no hope of ever finding your like on earth again! Help, we pray, by your intercession those whom you see encompassed by the taint of sin. Though you were already filled with the spirit of all the righteous, foreseeing the future and knowing the present, yet you always held before you the image of holy simplicity in order to shun all boastfulness.

But let us go back to what we were saying earlier and pick up the thread of the narrative.

NOTES

1 Giovanni Bonelli, who established the province of Provence in 1219. The chapter referred to was held in 1224 at Arles.
2 This is the great Portuguese theologian and preacher Fernando de Bulhoes, better known as St Anthony of Padua (where his relics are venerated). He was appointed by Francis as first Lector of Theology to the Order.
3 Psalm 19.10.
4 Riccerio of Muccia, who died in 1236 and was later venerated as a saint.

Chapter XIX

Francis' Care in Watching Over his Brothers;
His Contempt of Himself and His True Humility

———

51 When Francis rejoined his Brothers (whom he never left in spirit, as has been said) he conducted a thorough and scrupulous examination, investigating the conduct of each and every one of them. He was always motivated by a benign curiosity towards all his subordinates, and if he discovered that the slightest wrong had been done he would never leave it unpunished. First he would decide upon the spiritual failings, then pass judgement on bodily failings, and lastly he would root out all those occasions which open the door to sin. With all possible zeal and with all possible care he observed holy poverty ('Lady Poverty', as he called her), and fearing that he might find himself with needless possessions, he would not allow even a pot to remain in the house if he could do without it and somehow avoid being reduced to the direst need. (For he used to say that it was impossible to satisfy need without giving in to pleasure.) He scarcely ever, or only on the rarest occasions, allowed himself cooked food, and if he did, he would often mix it with ashes or pour cold water over it to spoil its flavour. How often, as he walked about the world preaching the gospel, he was invited to supper by great princes who loved and revered him, and he would taste a little meat, in order to observe the Holy Gospel,[1] then just pretend to eat the rest which, as he brought it to his mouth, he would surreptitiously drop into his lap. And what can I say of his drinking of wine, when he would not even allow himself to drink his fill of water when he was parched with thirst?

52 Whenever he accepted hospitality anywhere he would not allow blankets or bedspreads to be put down where he was to sleep. He laid his bare limbs on the bare ground with only his tunic for bedding, and when he did refresh his frail body in sleep,

he would often sleep in a sitting position, not lying down for a moment, using a piece of wood or a stone as a pillow. If he ever felt a craving for some particular food, as is only human, he could scarcely be persuaded to eat it when it was produced. Once, during a serious illness, he had eaten a small portion of chicken, and subsequently, after he had somewhat recovered his strength, he went to Assisi, and when he came to the city gate he told the Brother who was with him to tie a rope around his neck and drag him through the streets all round the city like a robber, and to shout at the top of his voice: 'Here! Come and see this glutton who has been stuffing himself with poultry behind your backs!' Of course, people flocked to see this extraordinary sight, but then they sighed and sighed again, and said as they wept together: 'What hope is there for us, whose whole lives are spent in bloodshed, who nourish our souls and bodies on immorality and drunkenness?' So their consciences were pricked, and Francis' shining example challenged them to lead better lives.

53 He did things of a similar sort on many occasions, both to show that he despised himself absolutely, and also to urge others to seek everlasting glory. He had become to himself 'like a broken vessel'[2] and was burdened by no fears or cares for his body; he actively put himself in the way of insults, lest he should be driven by love of self to desire some worldly thing. And being one who truly despised himself, Francis benefited everyone by teaching them by word and example to do the same.

The whole world sang his praises; with every justification they extolled him to the skies, and he alone thought himself the lowest of the low, he alone despised himself utterly. For when people paid him compliments it often caused him intense grief, and to keep this flattery at arm's length he would get somebody to insult him. He would call one of the Brothers over and say to him: 'I command you, on your obedience, to call me all the names you can think of: speak the truth and contradict the lies these people are telling.' And when this Brother, albeit unwillingly, called him a clod and a money-grubbing ne'er-do-well, Francis would smile and thank him warmly and reply: 'The Lord bless you for telling the real truth. That is just what the son of Pietro di Bernardone ought to be told.' And by talking in this way he would remind himself of his humble origins.

54 In fact, in order to show how completely contemptible he was, and to give the others an example of true confession, when he was guilty of some failing he was not ashamed to confess it before the whole congregation while he was preaching. What is more, if an evil thought about anyone entered his head or a hurtful remark chanced to escape his lips, he would immediately in all humility confess his sin to the person he had thought or spoken ill of, and beg his pardon. His conscience, which was witness to his total innocence, was constantly on guard, and would never allow him to rest until the mental wound had been soothed and healed. His yearning, certainly, was to progress in every kind of excellence, but not to draw attention to himself: to avoid falling into the sin of vanity, he shunned admiration in every way he could.

Alas for us who have lost you, reverend father, model of all goodness and humility! But in truth we have been judged justly, for we have lost one whom, when he was among us, we chose not to know.

NOTES

1 Jesus told his disciples: 'Eat such things as are set before you' (Luke 10.8), and this was embodied in the Franciscan Rule (II c.3).
2 Psalm 31.12.

———

Chapter XX

Francis' Longing to Receive Martyrdom as
He Went First to Spain Then to Syria; and
How God Saved the Sailors from Peril Through
Francis by Multiplying Their Provisions

55 Aglow with love for God, Francis was always eager to undertake dangerous missions; and as he followed the path of God's commandments in generosity of heart, he longed to attain the height of perfection. So in the sixth year of his conversion,[1] burning with desire for holy martyrdom, he decided to go abroad to the regions of Syria to preach repentance and the Christian faith to the Saracens and other unbelievers. He duly boarded a ship to sail there, but because of contrary winds he found himself with his fellow travellers in the region of Slavonia.[2] And after a while, seeing that he had been cheated of a chance to realize his great ambition, he begged some sailors who were heading for Ancona[3] to take him with them, since there was hardly any possibility of another ship sailing for Syria that year. They obstinately refused to take him because he had no money with which to pay them, but Francis, showing complete trust in the Lord's goodness, boarded their ship with his companions in secret. Then, by divine providence, and unbeknown to the sailors, a man came on board with all the necessary provisions. He found one of the crew who seemed a God-fearing man, and took him on one side and said: 'Take all these with you, and be sure to give them to the poor stowaways on board when they need them.' And so it was that when a heavy storm blew up and the crew after many days hard rowing had used up all their own supplies, only those of the pauper Francis were left. But through God's grace and power, these were increased to such an extent that, though the voyage lasted many more days, they were more than sufficient to supply the needs of everyone on board until they reached the port of Ancona. When the sailors realized that they had escaped a perilous

situation at sea through God's servant Francis, they gave thanks to Almighty God, who in his servants always shows himself worthy of wonder and love.

56 Francis, servant of God Most High, then left the sea and travelled the land, breaking it with the ploughshare of the Word, sowing the seeds of life, and bringing forth a blessed fruit. For at once, through the grace and will of the Most High, a succession of good and worthy men, both clergy and lay, wishing to flee the world and bravely crushing the devil, zealously followed Francis in his way of life. But though the vine shoot of the gospel can produce an abundance of choicest fruits of itself, nevertheless Francis' lofty ambition, his burning desire to win martyrdom never cooled for a moment, and before very long he set out for Morocco to preach the gospel of Christ to the Miramamolin[4] and his court. Francis so longed to get there that on occasion he would leave his companions behind and hurry on, like a man possessed, to achieve his purpose. But when he had got as far as Spain, the good Lord (who of his pure goodness saw fit to remember me and many others) stood in his path, and to stop him going any further caused him to abandon his journey by the threat of serious illness.

57 So Francis returned to the church of St Mary of the Portiuncula, and soon afterwards he was greatly cheered when other men came to join him, some of them scholars and some of noble birth.[5] Since he was of a most noble and discreet nature, Francis treated them all with proper respect, dutifully paying each of them the honour to which he was entitled. Indeed, he was endowed with exceptional sensitivity in such matters, and was always careful to show the respect due to people, whatever their rank. But still he could not rest without following the promptings of his saintly heart even more zealously, and in the thirteenth year of his conversion[6] he took one companion with him and journeyed to Syria, where every day the conflict between Christians and infidels grew grimmer and more bloodthirsty, and

57

St Francis Before the Sultan

Francis had to appear before the sultan of the Saracens.[7] But he had no fears.

How can one adequately tell of the unflinching courage Francis displayed as he stood before him, of his strength of spirit as he spoke, of his eloquence and confidence in replying to men who were insulting the law of Christ? Before he ever reached the sultan he had been captured by the sultan's men, humiliated and flogged, yet he was unafraid. He was threatened with torture and he showed no fear; death stared him in the face and he did not turn a hair. And though he had been treated appallingly by so many who felt nothing but hatred and hostility for him, yet he was received by the sultan with the greatest respect. The sultan paid him every possible honour; he offered him one gift after another in an attempt to seduce him with worldly riches. But when he saw that Francis was utterly resolute and regarded all such things as no better than dung, he was simply astonished and considered him unlike any other man on earth. He was deeply moved by what Francis said, and was more than willing to hear him out. But try as Francis might, the Lord did not grant him his desire for martyrdom. He was reserving for him the privilege of a favour that was unique.[8]

NOTES

1 The latter half of AD 1212.
2 A port on the Adriatic coast of Dalmatia.
3 A port on the Adriatic coast of central Italy, in the Marches (Le Marche).
4 The Sultan of Morocco, his proper title being *Emir el mumenin* ('head of the believers').
5 Celano himself may have been among their number.
6 Francis' trip to Syria was in 1219, so several years have been skipped here. Bonaventure tells us that his companion was Brother Illuminato.
7 The sultan was named Melek-el-Khamil. Francis appeared before the sultan during a short-lived truce between the warring parties.
8 The stigmata which Francis was to receive at La Verna in 1224.

Chapter XXI

His Preaching to the Birds; and the Obedience Wild Creatures Showed Him

58 While, as has been said, many were flocking to join the Brothers, Francis was journeying through the valley of Spoleto and reached a place near Bevagna[1] where an enormous number of different sorts of birds were gathered: there were doves,

and crows, and those the people call 'daws'. When Francis saw them, being an impulsive man and one who felt great tenderness towards all dumb creatures, he left his companions on the road and ran off towards them in a great surge of affection.

As he approached them, he realized that they were waiting for him, and he greeted them in his usual manner. To his great surprise they did not fly away, as birds do, and this filled him with happiness, and he humbly begged them to hear the word of God. After speaking to them at length he added:

My brother birds, you really ought to praise your Creator Lord and love him for ever: he has given you feathers for clothing, wings for flight, and everything you need. God has made you noble among his creatures: he has given you a home in the pure air of heaven, and though you neither sow nor reap he still protects and guides you, so that you have not a care in the world.

At this the little creatures showed their birdlike joy in a quite remarkable fashion, stretching their necks, spreading their wings and opening their beaks and gaping at him, and Francis went to and fro among them brushing their heads and bodies with his cloak. Finally he blessed them, and making the sign of the cross gave them leave to fly away elsewhere. Then the blessed father went on his way with his companions, rejoicing and giving thanks to God, whom all creatures humbly acknowledge and worship.

Having now by grace achieved a childlike simplicity (though he was not simple by nature) he began to accuse himself daily of negligence for not having preached to the birds before, since they had listened to the word of God with such reverence. So from that day on he would earnestly exhort all wild animals, birds, reptiles and even insensate creatures to praise and love their Creator, because every day, after calling on the Saviour's name, he learnt from personal experience that they would obey him.

59 One day he went to the city of Alviano[2] to preach the word of God, and there he climbed up a hillock so that

everyone could see him and asked for silence. But as the people stood waiting quietly and reverently, the silence was pierced by the twittering and chirping of a large flock of swallows which were building their nests there. And since Francis could not be heard by anyone above their din, he spoke to them. 'Sister swallows,' he said, 'it is now my turn to speak. You have already had quite enough to say. Listen to the word of the Lord and stay silent until my sermon is finished.' To the astonishment of all who stood there, the little birds at once fell silent, and did not move until the sermon was over. Everyone there was filled with awe at this miracle, and they said: 'This man truly is a saint, a friend of the Most High.' And with the deepest reverence they tried to touch him, or at least his clothes, praising and blessing God.

It is truly remarkable how even irrational creatures recognized his affection for them, and sensed the tenderness of his love.

60 Once, for example, when he was staying at the hill town of Greccio,[3] one of the Brothers brought him a live baby hare that had been caught in a snare. When the saint saw it he was moved with pity and said: 'Come to me, brother leveret. Why did you allow yourself to be caught out like this?' As soon as the hare was released by the Brother who was holding it, it took refuge with Francis and without any coaxing lay peacefully in his lap, knowing it was absolutely safe. And when it had rested there a while, Francis, stroking it with a mother's love, bade it farewell so that it could return to the woods. But the leveret, though placed time after time on the ground, kept running back to the saint's embrace until Francis finally had his Brothers carry it back to the wood nearby.

A similar thing happened with a rabbit (which is by nature a very wild creature) when Francis was on an island in the lake of Perugia.[4]

61 He was moved by the same compassion towards fish. When people caught fish, if he had the chance he would throw them back into the water, warning them to avoid being

caught next time. This happened when Francis was once on a boat near a harbour on the lake of Rieti[5] and a fisherman caught a splendid tench and respectfully offered it to Francis. Francis accepted it with pleasure, thanked the man, and at once began to address the fish as 'brother'. He then dropped it over the side of the boat and with deep devotion began to bless the name of the Lord; and as he prayed, the fish played in the water near the boat, never leaving the place where it had been dropped, until finally the saint finished his prayer and gave him leave to swim away. This is one example of how Francis, walking the path of obedience and taking upon himself the yoke of perfect submission, won great glory with God by making the wild creatures obey him.

He even turned water into wine, when he was in the throes of a grave illness once at the hermitage of St Urban.[6] And as soon as he had tasted it, he made such a speedy recovery that everyone considered it a miracle (as was in fact the case). And truly he is a saint when wild creatures obey him in this way, and at his will the very elements can be changed and put to other uses.

NOTES

1 In fact this happened at a place near Bevagna called Pian d'Arca, about three miles south of Assisi.
2 Alviano is about 30 miles south-west of Assisi, not far north of Orvieto.
3 Greccio is about 45 miles south of Assisi.
4 Lake Trasimene is meant, about 25 miles west of Assisi.
5 Rieti, a few miles south-east of Greccio, is about 40 miles north-east of Rome, and the lake is north-west of the city. This whole area is rich in associations with St Francis. He stayed at the nearby convent of La Foresta (north-east), and dictated the final Rule of his Order at Fonte Colombo (south-west).
6 St Urban (S. Urbano) is about six miles north-east of the hill town of Narni (Umbria).

Chapter XXII

His Preaching at Ascoli; and How the Sick were Healed in His Absence by Contact with Things Francis Had Touched

62 Around the time when Francis preached to the birds, as described above, while he was travelling about the cities and towns everywhere scattering the seeds of his blessing, he came to the city of Ascoli.[1] While he was preaching the word of God there, and speaking with his customary fervour, a change came over almost everyone who heard him and the right hand of the Most High filled them with such grace and devotion that they actually trampled on each other in their eagerness to hear and see him. It was at that time that 30 men, both clergy and lay, received the religious habit from him. Such was the faith of all who heard him, so great their devotion to God's saint, that anyone who could touch even the clothes he was wearing counted himself blessed.

Whenever he entered any city, the clergy were exultant, the bells rang out, the men leapt for joy, the women celebrated together, the children clapped their hands; and often people tore branches from the trees and went to meet him singing. The wickedness of heresy was confounded, the banner of faith was raised on high; and while the faithful were jubilant, the heretics went into hiding. So clear were the signs of holiness in Francis that no one dared speak against him, and the crowds had eyes for him alone. In the midst of all this and above all else, Francis maintained that the faith of the Holy Roman Church should be preserved, honoured and obeyed, the faith upon which alone depends the salvation of all who are to be saved. He revered priests, and indeed had the greatest affection for all ecclesiastical orders.

63 The people would offer him loaves to bless, then keep them for later use, and when they ate them they were cured of all kinds of ailments. Also, because of their great faith in him, they cut off bits of his tunic to keep, and did this so often that he was left all but naked. And, more remarkably, some were even cured of sickness by objects which Francis had touched with his hand. For example, there was a pregnant woman who lived in a village not far from Arezzo, and when the time came for her delivery, she was in labour for days on end and in such incredible pain that no one knew if she would live or die. Now the neighbours and relatives heard that Francis was going to pass by on his way to some hermitage, so they waited for him; but Francis happened to be riding a horse because he was weak and ill. When he reached the hermitage, he sent a Brother named Peter to take the horse back to the man who had been good enough to lend it to him. Brother Peter, in doing so, passed the house where the woman was suffering such agony. When the villagers saw him they ran towards him, thinking he was Francis, but when they saw he was not, they were heartbroken. Then finally they put their heads together and wondered if they could find anything Francis himself had touched, and after a long discussion they finally settled upon the reins he had held while riding. So they took the bit from the mouth of the horse Francis had been sitting on and laid the reins he had held on the woman: at once the danger passed and to her great joy she gave birth to her child in safety.

64 There was a man called Gualfreduccio who lived at Citta della Pieve.[2] He was a religious man who with all his household feared God and worshipped him, and he had in his possession a piece of cord Francis had once used as a girdle. Now it happened that in that region there were many men and women who suffered from a variety of sickness and fevers, and Gualfreduccio would visit the houses of the sick. He dipped the cord in water, or mixed some strands of it with water, then gave them a cupful to drink, and in Christ's name they were all made well again. These miracles took place in Francis' absence, these and many others which we could never recount in full, however long our narrative. But we will now give a short account of a few of

the things our Lord God deigned to do through Francis when he was physically present.

NOTES

1 Ascoli is in the Marches of Ancona (see Chapter XXVIII note 1) and about 20 miles from the coast.
2 Citta della Pieve is around 20 miles north-west of Orvieto, 40 miles north-north-west of Spoleto, and 40 miles west-south-west of Assisi.

———

Chapter XXIII

How He Cured a Cripple at Toscanella and a Paralytic at Narni

———

65 Once when Francis was travelling far afield to preach the gospel of God's kingdom, he came to a city called Toscanella.[1] While he was spreading the news of salvation here in his usual manner, he was given hospitality by a soldier of that city whose only son was a cripple, and totally disabled. He was a child past the age of weaning, but he still remained in his cradle. The boy's father, recognizing Francis' great holiness, threw himself humbly at his feet and begged him to cure his son. Francis, who considered himself of no use at all, and unworthy of such power and grace, for a long time refused to do it. Then at length he was overcome by the insistence of the father's entreaties. First he prayed, then laying his hand on the boy and blessing him he lifted him to his feet, and as everyone watched and rejoiced in the name of our Lord Jesus Christ, the boy stood erect, restored to perfect health, and began to walk about the house.

66 Once Francis was staying several days at Narni,[2] where there was a man called Peter who was paralysed and bedridden, and who for five months had been completely deprived of the use of his limbs, and could not get up at all or

move even an inch. He had lost all use of his feet and hands and head, and all he could do was move his tongue and open his eyes. But when he heard that Francis had come to Narni he sent a messenger to the bishop asking him, for the love of God, to send the saint to him, because he believed that just by seeing Francis and being in his presence he would be delivered from his affliction. And so it happened. Francis went to him, made the sign of the cross all over him from head to foot, and at once completely rid him of his sickness and made him as well again as he had ever been.

NOTES

1 Toscanella (since 1911 Tuscania) is a little walled town 11 miles west of Viterbo, about ten miles south of the Lago di Bolsena.
2 Narni is a hill town standing on the Via Flaminia 20 miles north-west of Rieti, about seven miles south-west of Terni.

———

Chapter XXIV

How He Restored the Sight of a Blind Woman, and Cured Another Woman with Crippled Hands at Gubbio

———

67 A woman, also of Narni, had been struck blind. Francis made the sign of the cross over her eyes and she was at once blessed with the miracle she had longed for, and could see again.

At Gubbio there was a woman whose hands were both so rigidly clenched that she could do nothing with them. As soon as she learned that the saint had come to Gubbio, she ran to him, and with an expression of utter misery and dejection on her face showed him her misshapen hands and repeatedly begged him to be good enough to touch them. Francis was moved with compassion: he touched her hands and healed her. The woman was jubilant, and at once went home and made him a cheesecake with her own hands, and offered it to the saint. He accepted a little out of charity, then told her to share the rest out at home with her family.

———

Chapter XXV

How He Saved a Brother from the Falling Sickness, or from a Demon; and How He Cured a Woman Possessed of a Demon at the City of San Gemini

———

68 One of the Brothers suffered frequently from a terrible affliction that was alarming to observe. (I cannot give a name to the condition, but some believe it was demonic possession.) He would often collapse, then with a terrible look in his eye he would roll about foaming at the mouth; one moment his body was contracted into a ball, the next his limbs sprawled everywhere; sometimes they were knotted and twisted, sometimes rigid and immoveable. At times, tense and rigid all over, he was catapulted about six feet into the air, with his feet reaching the height of his head, and then he would suddenly fall back to the ground again. Francis was moved to pity by his terrible affliction, so he went to the Brother, said a prayer, made the sign of the cross over him and blessed him. At once he was cured, and he was never troubled again in the slightest by this illness.

69 One day when Francis was passing through the diocese of Narni he came to the town of San Gemini,[1] and while he was preaching the gospel there he was entertained, together with three of his Brothers, by a man who feared and worshipped God, and whose reputation stood high in the area. But his wife, as was known to everyone who lived thereabouts, was tormented by an evil spirit. So her husband asked Francis to help her, trusting that

through his merits his wife could be cured. But Francis, desiring in his simplicity to be despised rather than to win worldly acclaim through public displays of sanctity, absolutely refused to do this. At length, however, because God was watching over the affair, and so many people insistently begged him for help, Francis yielded to their entreaties. He called the three Brothers who were with him and putting each of them in a corner of the house said to them: 'Let us pray to the Lord for this woman, brothers, asking that God may shake the devil's yoke from her shoulders to his praise and glory. Let us stand apart in the four corners of the house: we must not let the evil spirit escape us or fool us by hiding in the recesses.' He then prayed, and when he had finished, full of the power of the Holy Spirit, Francis went to the woman, who was in terrible torment and crying out horribly, and said: 'In the name of our Lord Jesus Christ I command you to obey me, evil spirit, and to leave this woman, and never dare to trouble her again.' Scarcely had he finished speaking when the demon came out, and came out so swiftly and with such a furious roar that Francis thought he must be imagining things, so sudden was the woman's release, and so instant the demon's obedience. And Francis left at once with a blush of shame, for providence had worked in such a way that he had no possible grounds for vainglory.

Francis was passing through the same place on another occasion in the company of Brother Elias, and as soon as the woman he had healed learnt of his arrival, up she got and ran through the street after him, begging him to speak to her. But Francis, realizing that it was the woman from whom he had once cast out a demon by the power of God, did not want to speak to her. But she kept kissing the prints his feet had made, giving thanks to God and his servant Francis, who had saved her when she was at death's door. Finally Brother Elias prevailed upon him, and Francis did speak to her, but only after a number of people had assured him that she had indeed been possessed, and that she was now completely cured.[2]

1 San Gemini is 30 miles south-west of Assisi, and some five miles north-west of Terni.
2 Francis' caution and suspicion here is a little puzzling. Perhaps he feared that the woman might still be possessed and was trying to bring the matter to public notice. In fact she merely wanted to thank him because she had been completely cured, and it was when Elias reassured him about her intention that he relented and spoke to her.

Chapter XXVI

How He also Cast Out a Demon at Citta di Castello

70 At Citta di Castello[1] there was a woman possessed by an evil spirit, and when Francis was there this woman was brought to the house where he was staying. But she remained outside, and began to gnash her teeth, make terrible faces and howl with ghastly laughter, as happens in cases of demonic possession. Many of the townsfolk, both men and women, came to Francis and begged him to help her, for the evil spirit had tormented her for some time now and had troubled them too by his screaming. Francis then sent her the Brother who was accompanying him to find out whether it really was a demon, or merely a woman's pretence. As soon as the woman saw this Brother she began to mock him, knowing he was not the saint at all. Meanwhile inside the house Francis was at prayer, and when he had finished, he came out, and the woman began to tremble and to roll upon the ground, unable to withstand his power. Francis called her to him and said: 'I order you to obey me, unclean spirit, and leave her.' The evil spirit at once left her without doing her further harm, and departed in great fury. Thanks be to God, whose power is everywhere beyond measure.

But since it is not our intention to describe miracles (which do not produce sanctity, but simply manifest it) but rather the exemplary life Francis led and its perfect holiness, we shall pass over the many other miracles he performed and survey his efforts to save souls.

NOTE

1 Citta di Castello is 20 miles east of Arezzo, and 25 miles north of Perugia.

━━

Chapter XXVII

His Singlemindedness and Unwavering
Resolution; His Preaching before Pope Honorius;
and How He Committed Himself and
His Brothers to the Patronage of Lord Hugo,
Bishop of Ostia

━━

71 Francis had been taught to seek not his own good, but whatever he thought was expedient for the salvation of others. But above all he longed for bodily dissolution and union with Christ, so his chief desire was to be free from everything in the world, so that the serenity of his mind might not be troubled even for a moment by the taint of any earthly defilement. He made himself insensible to the clamour of all outward things, and checking all his outward senses by an immense effort of will and suppressing his natural instincts, he gave himself up to God alone. He built his nest in the cleft of a rock and his dwelling was in a hollow of the wall.[1] And fertile indeed were the long hours he spent wandering lonely places where, wholly lost to himself he would rest long hours in the wounds of the Saviour. So he often chose to be in solitary places where he might concentrate totally upon God: yet, when he saw the time was right, he was not slow to apply himself to the affairs of others, and would devote himself wholeheartedly to the salvation of his neighbours. His safest haven was prayer, and not the prayer of a moment, not thoughtless,

70

absent-minded or presumptuous prayer, but long-sustained prayer, prayer full of devotion and quiet humility. If he began late in the day, he had hardly finished by morning. Walking, sitting, eating and drinking, Francis was always engrossed in prayer. He would go off alone at night to pray in derelict churches or those which stood in remote places, and there, with God's grace as protection, he mastered many fears and anxieties.

72 He fought hand-to-hand with the devil, who not only assailed him inwardly with temptations in such places, but terrified him also with the sudden collapse and ruin of the buildings around him. But Francis, valiant champion of Christ, knowing that his Lord was everywhere omnipotent, yielded to no terrors, but said in his heart: 'You can no more brandish the arms of your wickedness against me here, evil one, than if we were in a crowded public place, with everyone looking on.' Truly, Francis was utterly unwavering in resolve, and he had no thought for anything other than the Lord's work. Though he might be speaking before many thousands of people (as happened very often) he was as relaxed as if he were speaking to one dear friend. He treated a vast gathering of people as one man, and he preached with the same painstaking care to one man as if it were to a crowd. This confidence in speaking came from his purity of mind; and without planning what to say he would say wonderful things no one had heard before. Then again sometimes, if he had given some thought to his sermon beforehand, when the crowds gathered he could not remember what he had planned and had nothing to say. But without any embarrassment he would confess to the people that there were lots of things he had planned to say, but he could remember absolutely none of them; then all of a sudden he would be inspired with such eloquence that he amazed everyone who heard him. But on other occasions when he could find nothing to say, he simply dismissed the people with his blessing, well aware that this alone served them as well as the lengthiest sermon.

73 Once Francis went to Rome on a matter concerning the Order, and was longing for the chance to speak before Pope Honorius[2] and the venerable cardinals. But when Hugo[3] Bishop of Ostia learnt of this, he was filled with both joy and unease; he revered the saint and regarded him with deep affection, but while he admired his zeal, he was also aware of his innocence and naivety. But confident in the mercy of Almighty God, which in times of need never fails those who devoutly trust in it, he took Francis before the pope and the cardinals. There Francis stood before all these great dignitaries, and after receiving the pope's permission and his blessing, he boldly began to speak. He spoke with such spiritual fervour that he could not contain himself for joy, and with each word he uttered he kept moving his feet as if he were dancing – not in a sensual way, but because he was ablaze with the fire of divine love; and it made no one laugh – on the contrary, it wrung tears of grief from them. Many of those present were pierced to the heart as they observed God's grace in Francis and marvelled at his unwavering conviction. But all this time the Bishop of Ostia was in a terrible state of suspense, and he prayed with all his heart to the Lord that Francis might not be despised for his simplicity (since his success or failure reflected upon himself, now he had been appointed patron[4] of Francis' community).

74 For Francis had looked to Hugo as a son to his father, as an only child to his mother, sleeping and resting securely in the bosom of his clemency. And indeed Hugo performed all the duties and did all the work expected of a shepherd for Francis and his flock, though he left the title of 'pastor' to the saint himself.

Francis made the provisions necessary for his brothers, but the happy bishop put those provisions into effect. Ah, how many, especially at its very beginning, plotted to destroy the new foundation! How many tried to smother the choice new vine which the Lord in his unfailing kindness was planting in the world! How many strove to steal and to consume its first and purest fruits! But they were all slain by the sword of this reverend bishop and father, and their efforts were confounded. Hugo was a fount of eloquence, a pillar of the Church, a champion of truth, and a lover of the humble. So it was a lucky and momentous day when Francis entrusted himself to the patronage of the venerable bishop.

They first became friends when Bishop Hugo was Legate of the Apostolic See in Tuscany (an office he often held) and Francis, who had not yet many followers and was planning a visit to France, arrived in Florence, where the bishop was then in residence. They were not yet bound by any special intimacy, but each knew of the other's reputation for holiness and this alone united them in mutual affection and goodwill.[5]

75 Since it was Francis' custom upon entering any city or province to call upon its bishop or priest, when he heard of the presence of so important a pontiff as Hugo, he presented himself before him with great reverence. And when Bishop Hugo saw him, he received him with the humble devotion he always showed to those who professed holy religion, and especially those who bore the noble ensign of poverty and simplicity. And because he was always anxious to provide for the needs of the poor and to deal with their concerns with special care, he made sure to ask Francis the reason for his coming, and listened to his proposal most attentively. When he saw that Francis despised worldly things more than any other man, and was glowing with that fire which Jesus sent into the world, from that moment his soul was one with Francis' soul, and he earnestly entreated his prayers, and was most happy to offer him his protection in whatever he did. Accordingly he advised him not to proceed on the journey he had begun, but to devote every waking hour to caring for and watching over those whom the Lord God had entrusted to him. And Francis, seeing how kindly the bishop was disposed towards him, how warm his affection was, and how shrewd his advice, was

quite overjoyed. He at once fell at his feet, and with all his heart committed and entrusted himself and his brothers to him.

NOTES

1 Compare Song of Solomon 2.14.

2 Honorius III was pope from 1216 to 1227, and it was he who gave the final confirmation of St Francis' Rule in 1223.

3 See Prologue to Part I, note 1. Hugo was Celano's hero, as he was Francis' hero. The cardinal was undoubtedly a good man, but he was also a courtier and a politician, and his vision of what the Order should be hardly accorded with its founder's. He wanted organization and control, not anarchy and poverty (leading to possible extinction), and in imposing his will he inevitably did some violence to the Franciscan ideal of mendicant simplicity.

4 Hugo became the first Protector of the Order around 1220.

5 The precise chronology of the friendship between Francis and Hugo is uncertain. It is at least possible that, when they met at Florence, Hugo had already been appointed protector of the Order, and in dissuading Francis from his proposed mission to France, was exercising his official powers.

Chapter XXVIII

His Fervent Charity and Compassion Towards the Poor; and His Rescue of a Sheep and Some Lambs

76 Francis the poor, the father of the poor, who made himself in every way like the poor, was troubled if he saw anyone poorer than himself, not from any longing for worldly renown, but simply from a feeling of compassion. And though he was himself content with a poor, rough tunic, he many times offered to share it with some pauper. But so that this richest of poor men might show the deep pity he felt and help the poor at least to some degree, he would go begging among the rich of this world in the freezing cold, and ask them to lend him a cloak or some furs. And when in their devotion they promised to do so almost

before he had made his request, Francis would tell them: 'I will accept this from you on the understanding that you never expect to get it back again.' Then he would happily and triumphantly clothe the first poor man he met with whatever he had been given. He was exceedingly distressed if he saw any poor person being abused, or if he heard anyone utter a curse at any creature.

It once happened that one of the Brothers had rebuked a poor man who was begging alms. 'Suppose you are rich,' he said, 'and just pretending to be poor!' When Francis, the father of the poor, heard of this he was deeply distressed. He severely reprimanded the Brother who had made the remark, and ordered him to strip himself naked before the poor man, kiss his feet and beg his pardon. For, as he always used to say: 'Anyone who abuses a pauper is wronging Christ, for the pauper bears the noble image of Christ, who made himself poor in this world for our sake.' So when he found poor folk bowed down with wood or other heavy loads, he often put his own shoulder beneath the burden to help them, however feeble he might be.

77 Francis overflowed with charity, and he felt pity not only for men in need, but also for dumb animals, reptiles, birds, and all other creatures, whatever their intelligence. But of all the animal kingdom those Francis loved most dearly and most spontaneously were little lambs, because in the Holy Scriptures the humility of our Lord Jesus Christ is most frequently likened to and most aptly compared with that of a lamb. Francis was never happier than when embracing or contemplating something in which he could find a hidden similarity to the Son of God.

Once he travelled through the Marches of Ancona[1] and after preaching the word of God there, he had set out for Osimo[2] with Brother Paul, whom he had appointed as minister of all the Brothers in that province,[3] and in the fields he found a shepherd grazing a herd of nanny goats and billy goats. And among the milling herd there was one little sheep, humbly going about its business and peacefully grazing. When Francis saw it he stopped;

75

touched to the quick, he said with a deep groan to the Brother who was with him: 'Do you see this sheep walking about so meekly among these goats? I tell you, our Lord Jesus Christ was as meek and humble when he walked among the Pharisees and chief priests. So I beg you, my son, for love of him, take pity on this little sheep as I do. Let us buy it and rescue it from this herd of goats.'

78 Brother Paul was first surprised at Francis' distress, and then began to share his grief. But they had nothing but the shabby tunics they were wearing, and were worrying about how they might find the money when up came a travelling merchant who promptly offered them the amount they wanted. Giving thanks to God they took the sheep and went on to Osimo. There they called on the bishop and were received by him with great respect. His lordship, however, was taken aback by the sheep which the saint had in tow and by the affection he showed it. But when Francis recounted to him at length the parable of the sheep in the Gospel the bishop was deeply touched and gave thanks to God for a saint so pure. The following day Francis left Osimo and, wondering what he should do with the sheep, he took the advice of his companion and handed it over to a community of nuns at San Severino.[4] These honoured handmaids of Christ were delighted to receive the sheep, which they regarded as a wonderful gift, a gift from God himself. They kept it with great care for a long time and wove a tunic from its wool which they sent to Francis when he was presiding over a chapter of the Order at St Mary of the Portiuncula. Francis was overjoyed: he received the tunic with humble gratitude and embraced and kissed it, inviting all who were with him to share his happiness.

79 On another occasion when he was passing through the same area in the Marches with the same Brother eagerly accompanying him, he met a man with two little lambs trussed up and hanging over his shoulder that he was taking to market to sell. When Francis heard the lambs bleating he was moved to pity, and he went up and caressed them like a mother showing pity for her weeping child. And he said to the man: 'Why are you carrying my brother lambs about trussed up like that and causing them such suffering?' The man replied: 'I have to, for I need the money.' 'What will happen to them then?' asked the saint. 'Whoever buys them will kill them and eat them,' the man replied. 'No, no,' Francis cried, 'God forbid! Take this cloak I am wearing in exchange for them and give the lambs to me.' The man was only too willing to give Francis the lambs and to take his cloak, because it was worth much more (in fact Francis had borrowed it that very day from one of the faithful to keep out the cold). But then, after he had bought the lambs, the saint began to wonder what he should do with them and, on the advice of the Brother who was with him, he gave them back to the man to keep, instructing him never to sell them or do them harm, but to feed them and care for them and do everything he could to ensure their well being.

NOTES

1 The Marches (Le Marche) are north-east of Assisi lying along the Adriatic coast. Ancona itself is an important port, about 65 miles from Assisi.

2 Osimo is a few miles south of Ancona.

3 The Marches of Ancona were a province in the Order: when the chapter met at the Portiuncula in 1217, Italy was divided into six provinces: Tuscany, Lombardy, The Marches of Ancona, Terra di Lavoro (south of Rome), Apulia and Calabria. The chapter also appointed ministers to supervise the friars in each province.

4 That is, the monastery of Poor Clares near San Severino, which is some 30 miles south-west of Ancona.

77

Chapter XXIX

The Love Francis Felt for All Creatures for Their Creator's Sake. A Description of the Saint's Spiritual and Physical Characteristics

———

80 It would take too long and indeed it would be impossible to recount everything Francis did, and to summarize all he taught in his lifetime. Who could ever express the intensity of the love he felt for everything in God's creation? Who could describe the delight he experienced when contemplating the wisdom, power and goodness of the Creator in his creatures? Truly he was very often filled with a mysterious, unutterable joy when he considered the sun, or beheld the moon, or gazed at the stars and heavens. Ah, such innocent holiness, such holy innocence! He was afire with love even for little worms, because he knew the psalm which alludes to the Saviour with the words: 'I am a worm and no man'.[1] So he would gather them up from the road and put them somewhere safe so they should not be trodden on by passers-by. And what shall I say about his love for all the other lower creatures, when he provided bees with honey or the best wine in winter to keep them from dying of the cold? And his admiration for their efficiency and skill was so boundless that he would often spend a whole day singing their praises and those of other creatures, to the glory of God. Just as in ancient times the three youths in the burning, fiery furnace invited all the elements to laud and glorify the Creator of the universe,[2] so Francis, filled with the Spirit of God, never ceased glorifying, praising and blessing the Creator and Governor of all things in all the elements and creatures.[3]

81 Imagine the joy that beautiful flowers gave him, when he saw the elegance of their shape and caught the fragrance of their perfume. For he at once turned in his mind's eye to contemplation of the beauty of that bright flower which came forth

in springtime from the root of Jesse and with its fragrance has raised countless thousands of the dead. And whenever he came upon a whole host of flowers, he would preach to them and invite them to praise the Lord as if they were rational creatures. So it was with cornfields and vineyards, rocks and woods, and all the beauties of the fields, splashing fountains, lush, green gardens, earth and fire, air and wind – all these Francis would, in complete sincerity, urge to love God and to serve him with gladness. In short, he called all creatures by the name of 'brother', and he had an extraordinary gift, an intuitive understanding of the secrets of nature which was denied to other men, for he had already escaped all earthly bonds and found glorious freedom as one of the children of God.[4]

And now, sweet Jesus, he who on earth always taught all creatures that you are a God of love, now with the angels in heaven praises you as a God of wonder.

82 For whenever he uttered your name, Holy Lord, he was filled with emotions past human understanding, his whole being was transported with joy, he was filled with purest bliss; indeed he seemed to become a new man, someone from another world. And whenever he found a piece of paper with writing on it, whether sacred or profane, by the wayside, in a house or on the ground, he would pick it up with the utmost care and put it in some consecrated place, or somewhere safe, in case the Lord's name, or something to do with the Lord's name might be written on it. Once when one of the Brothers asked him why he was so careful to pick up the writings even of pagans or writings where there was no reference to the Lord's name, Francis answered: 'Because, my son, they still contain the letters which make up the glorious name of the Lord God. The good that is there does not belong to the pagans or to any other men, but to God alone, from whom all good comes.' And equally remarkable is the fact that whenever he dictated letters, whether of greeting or reproof, he would not allow any corrections even of the most common

errors, when letters or syllables were superfluous or had been left out.

83 What a fine, shining, glorious example Francis was in his innocence of life: in his simple way of speaking, in his purity of heart, in his love of God, in his charity towards his brothers, in his fervent obedience, willing submission, and the angelic expression he wore! His manners were charming, his disposition was mild, his way of talking courteous; he was most apt in exhortation, most faithful in performing any service with which he was charged, shrewd in counsel, competent in administration, and gracious in all things. Serene, sweet-natured, sober, he was rapt in contemplation, assiduous in prayer, and zealous in all things. He was unwavering in purpose, resolute in virtue, persevering in grace, the same in all things. He was swift to forgive and slow to anger; he was quick-witted, had a tenacious memory, was subtle in argument, cautious in decision-making, and simple in all things. He was severe on himself, kind to others, and discreet in all things.

Francis was a most eloquent man, and a man with a cheerful and kindly face; he knew nothing of cowardice, and was devoid of arrogance. He was of medium height, inclining to shortness; his head was of normal size and round, his face rather long and prominent, his forehead unlined and narrow; his eyes were of average size, black, with a frank look; his hair was dark, his eyebrows straight, his nose even, thin and straight; his ears were pointed, but small; his temples smooth. The words he spoke were kindly, but could be fiery and penetrating. His voice was powerful, but melodious, clear and resonant. His teeth were close-set, even and white; his lips were delicate and thin, his beard was black and on the sparse side, his neck slender, his shoulders straight, his arms short, his hands slender, with long, tapering fingers and nails; his legs were thin, his feet tiny; his skin delicate, his flesh very spare.[5] He wore rough clothing, he slept very little, he gave with great generosity. And because he was so very humble, he displayed absolute meekness to all men, and could adapt himself to suit their different behaviour.

Among the holy he was holier still: among sinners, he was as one of them.

So most holy father, lover of sinners, in your great goodness and by your illustrious intercession raise up, we beg you, all those you see wallowing miserably in the mire of their transgressions.

NOTES

1   Psalm 22.6.
2   Daniel 3.
3   The author is surely thinking of *The Canticle of Brother Sun* (composed during Francis' last illness at St Damian's in 1225), a poem in Umbrian dialect praising God for the moon and stars, the wind and air, water and fire and earth.
4   See Romans 8.21.
5   Thomas of Celano knew Francis well, but his description here is unlike most extant portraits of the saint. The traditional image of Francis is of a skeletonic, pale-faced ascetic, but probably the earliest authentic portrait (at Subiaco, and dated 1223, which would mean that it was done during the saint's lifetime) shows a cowled, bearded monk with a disarmingly ordinary face, but a face full of humanity and compassion.

Chapter XXX

The Crib He Made on the Day of the Lord's Birth

84 His primary intention, his chief desire and his supreme purpose was in all things and through all things to observe the Holy Gospel, and with all possible care and devotion, with all the longing of his mind and all the fervour of his heart to obey the teaching of our Lord Jesus Christ and follow in his footsteps. He would meditate endlessly upon his words and consider his actions with the most painstaking care. Chiefly it was Christ's humility in his incarnation, and the love he showed in his passion that occupied his mind – so much so indeed that he could scarcely

81

think about anything else. Therefore what he did at the hill town of Greccio on the birthday of Our Lord Jesus Christ in the third year before his glorious death should be recorded and remembered with reverence.[1]

At Greccio there was a man called John who had a good name, and lived an even better life, for whom Francis had a particular affection, because though he had been one of the most noble and highly respected men in his town, he had trodden worldly nobility underfoot and gone after nobility of soul. Now about a fortnight before the Lord's nativity Francis sent for John, as he often did, and said to him:

If you would like to celebrate the Lord's birthday with me at Greccio, go there ahead of me and be sure to get things ready as I tell you. I want to keep the memory of the child's birth in Bethlehem in such a way that I can somehow see before me the hardships of his infancy, see the babe lying in the manger on the hay where he was laid, with the ox and the ass standing by.

As soon as John heard this, good and faithful soul that he was, he went off to Greccio as quickly as he could, and got everything ready as the saint had dictated.

85 The day of rejoicing approached, the time of celebration was at hand. The Brothers were summoned from their various communities and the men and women of Greccio with happy hearts got ready all the candles and torches they could to brighten the night which has brightened all the days and years since with its radiant star. Finally Francis arrived and was delighted to find everything ready. And indeed a manger had been found, hay fetched, and an ox and an ass were led in. There simplicity was honoured, poverty exalted, humility glorified. Greccio became, as it were, a new Bethlehem.

The night was made as bright as day, a delight to men and beasts alike. The people all came to see and were thrilled at this new mystery as never before. The woods resounded with voices, the rocks echoed back the sounds of rejoicing. The Brothers sang, giving due praises to the Lord, and the whole night rang with sounds of jubilation. The saint stood before the crib sighing deeply, overwhelmed with love, and filled with a wondrous joy. A solemn mass was celebrated over the crib and the priest enjoyed a consolation he had never known before.

86 Francis wore the vestments of a deacon (for he had been admitted to that order) and chanted the Gospel with

St Francis Rocking the Bambino at Greccio

sonorous voice. And with this powerful, melodious, clear and resonant voice of his he invited everyone to receive the rewards of heaven. Then he preached to the people gathered round, and spoke honey-sweet words about the nativity of the pauper king and the little town of Bethlehem. And often when he was going to utter the name of Jesus Christ he was so ablaze with love that he would call him the Child of Bethlehem, and as he spoke the word Bethlehem it sounded like a sheep bleating, and though the sound came from his mouth, it flowed rather from his whole being, which was bursting with tenderness. Also, when he mentioned the Child of Bethlehem or called Jesus by name, he seemed almost to lick his lips, as if he were relishing the taste of the words, and savouring their sweetness.

That night at Greccio the Almighty granted many blessings, and one man had a vision of miraculous power. He saw, lying lifeless in the manger, a little boy, and then he watched Francis go up to the child and rouse him as it were from the drowsiness of sleep. And this vision was not wide of the mark, because the child Jesus had been consigned to oblivion in the hearts of many people, people in whom, through the working of his grace, he was raised to life again through his servant Francis, and imprinted unforgettably upon their memories.

At length the solemn vigil came to an end and everyone returned happily home.

87 The hay which had been in the manger was kept, so that through it the Lord in his mercy might save beasts of burden and other animals from sickness. And so indeed it came about, and many animals suffering from a variety of diseases in the neighbourhood were cured of their sicknesses when they ate the hay. What is more, women who were in protracted and painful labour were safely delivered if they placed some of the hay on their bodies. Also a great number of people of either sex suffering from various complaints regained their health in the same way.

Finally, the place where the manger had stood was consecrated as a temple to the Lord, and over the crib an altar was built and a church was dedicated in honour of St Francis; so that where once beasts had eaten their fodder of hay, thereafter men might, for the health of their souls and bodies, eat the flesh of the pure and spotless Lamb, our Lord Jesus Christ, who with supreme and ineffable charity gave himself for us, and with the Father and the Holy Spirit lives and reigns, God eternally glorious, for all ages to come. Amen. Alleluia, Alleluia.

NOTE

1 Greccio is about 45 miles south of Assisi. The year was 1223.

End of First Part of the Life and Acts of St Francis

PART II

Here Begins the Second Part,
Concerning the Last Two Years of
the Life of our Most Blessed Father Francis
and his Happy Death

Chapter I

The Contents of This Book;
the Time of Francis' Death, and
His Progress in Perfection

——

88 In the first part (which by the Saviour's grace we have brought to a fitting conclusion) we gave a description, such as it is, of the life and acts of St Francis up to the eighteenth year of his conversion.[1] We will now briefly append to that the most accurate account we have been able to obtain of the rest of his acts, starting from the penultimate year of his life. For the present we intend to include only those things which appear most important, so that those who wish to say more about them may still be able to find additional material.

In the 1226th year of our Lord's incarnation, in the fourteenth indiction,[2] on Sunday 4 October,[3] our most blessed father Francis left the prison of the flesh and soared happily to the abodes of the heavenly spirits, thus perfecting what he had begun. He died at St Mary of the Portiuncula in the city of Assisi where he first established the Order of Friars Minor, 20 years from the date when he had first devoted his life to Christ and followed in the life and footsteps of the apostles. To hymns and songs of praise his sacred and hallowed body was laid to rest and honourably buried in that same city, where it is radiant with glory for the many miracles it works to the glory of the Almighty. Amen.

89 Since Francis had had little or no instruction in the religious life and in the knowledge of God when he was young, he remained for some considerable time a prey to his natural instincts and vices; but he was freed from sin by a change worked in him by the right hand of the Most High and by the grace and power

of the Most High he was filled with divine wisdom above all others of his time. For when the teachings of the gospel had as a whole (though not of course in every respect) proved ineffective everywhere, Francis was sent by God to bear witness to the truth throughout the whole world, following the example of the apostles. And so it came about that his teaching showed that all the wisdom of this world is most evidently foolishness, and in a short space of time he converted it, under Christ's guidance, to the true wisdom of God by the 'foolishness' of his preaching.[4] For this latter-day evangelist, like one of the rivers of paradise, has lovingly bathed the whole earth in the waters of the gospel, and preached the way of the Son of God and the doctrine of truth by showing it in practice. Through Francis, therefore, the world was filled with unexpected happiness and spiritual renewal, and a new shoot of the ancient religion lent new vigour to souls that had become hardened and old. A new spirit was given to the hearts of the elect, and the oil of salvation was poured out in their midst when, like one of the luminaries of heaven, Francis, Christ's servant and saint, shone gloriously from above with a new rite and with new marvels.[5] Through him the miracles of ancient times were seen again, while in the desert of this world, by a new order but in the ancient way, a fruitful vine was planted, a vine with sweet flowers breathing the fragrance of holy virtues by extending everywhere the tendrils of a sacred religion.

90 For though Francis was a man subject to the same weaknesses as we are, he was not content to live according to the common precepts, but overflowing with the most fervent charity he took the path of total perfection; he reached for the heights of perfect holiness, and attained the summit of all perfection. So every type of person of whatever age or sex has in Francis a clear illustration of the path to salvation and shining examples of holiness in action. Any who intend to embrace the life of hardship and strive eagerly after the superior gifts of the more excellent way, should look into the mirror of his life and they will learn all perfection.

If any, fearing the steep ascent to the summit of the mountain, take the lower and easier way, on this level, too, they will find in him the appropriate guidance. If any, finally, look for signs and wonders, they should ask it of his holiness and they will get what they desire.

And indeed Francis' glorious life sheds a brighter light on the perfection of the saints of earlier times. The passion of Jesus Christ proves this, and his cross makes it most abundantly clear. For it is a fact that the venerable father was marked on five parts of his body with the signs of Christ's cross and passion, just as if he had hung on the cross with the Son of God. This is a profound mystery and reveals the majesty of special love. But in it a secret purpose lies hidden, in it a solemn mystery is concealed which we believe is known to God alone, and was in part disclosed by the saint himself to one person. There seems, therefore, no point in attempting much in praise of one whose praise comes from him who is the Praise of all, the Source of all, and the Highest Honour of all, bestowing the prerogatives of light.[6] So, blessing the one holy, true and glorious God, let us return to our narrative.

NOTES

1 That is, AD 1224.
2 The 'indiction' was a cycle of 15 years, and the number given to the indiction indicates the year within the cycle. The author is using the papal method of calculation: three is added to the year AD, and the sum is divided by fifteen. This therefore was the fourteenth year of the eighty-second cycle.
3 According to our reckoning Francis died on Saturday 3 October. But according to ancient reckoning, day ran from evening to evening; so, since Francis died about an hour after dark, Sunday 4 October had already begun, and that is Francis' feast day.
4 See 1 Corinthians 1.21.
5 Note the recurrent motif of 'renewal' here and elsewhere. Francis brought a fresh style and a new approach to the living of the gospel: he was different and original. Note also that the author is at pains to point out that Francis' new movement was quite in accord with ancient practices: in fact ancient truths were simply being presented in a new way.

6 A cryptic phrase. Celano has been talking about the mystery of the stigmata, and may here be referring to God as the granter of such extraordinary prerogatives.

Chapter II

Francis' Greatest Desire; and How He Understood the Lord's Will Towards Him Through the Opening of a Book

91 One day Francis forsook the crowds of people who were daily gathering with the greatest devotion to hear and see him and went to a quiet, secret and lonely place, wishing to give himself wholly to God there, and to cleanse himself of any dust that might have clung to him from his association with the world. It was his practice to divide the time given to him for the winning of grace and, as he thought fit, to devote part of it to the profit of his neighbours, and to spend the rest in blessed seclusion and contemplation. So he took with him very few companions, those who were more familiar with his holy way of life than the rest, so that they could ensure his privacy and protect him from disturbances, and generally do all they could to preserve his peace and quiet.

When Francis had remained in his retreat for some time, and through constant prayer and frequent contemplation had attained to an indescribable intimacy with God, he conceived a desire to know what he could do or suffer that would be most acceptable to the eternal King. He most earnestly sought to discover, and in all humility he longed to know in what way he might perfectly unite his will with that of God, what path he should take, what goal he should pursue that would be most in accordance with his plan and the gracious purpose of his will. This was always his highest philosophy, this was always his most burning desire throughout his life: to find out from the simple and wise, from the perfect and imperfect alike how he might attain to the way of truth and finally fulfil his highest purpose.

92 For though he was the most perfect of the perfect, he rejected any idea that he might be perfect and thought himself utterly imperfect. For he had tasted and seen how sweet, how delightful and 'how good the God of Israel is to those who are of upright heart'¹ and seek him in pure simplicity and true purity. Indeed, the distillations of sweetness and delight that he felt breathed on him from above (a gift rarely bestowed on even the rarest of men) compelled him to renounce himself utterly, and filled as he was with such bliss he longed with every part of his being to pass over wholly to the sphere where, in ecstasy, he had already in part gone before. Filled with the spirit of God, Francis was ready to suffer any mental anguish and to endure any physical suffering if only his wish might finally be granted, that the will of his Heavenly Father might mercifully be fulfilled in him. So one day he went before the holy altar which had been built in the hermitage where he was staying, and picked up a volume in which the Holy Gospel was written and placed it reverently on the altar. Then he prostrated himself in prayer to God (a prayer in his heart as well as on his lips) and humbly asked that God, 'the father of mercies and God of all comfort'² would be graciously pleased to reveal his will to him. And so that he might be able perfectly to finish what he had earlier begun in simplicity and devotion, he humbly prayed that he might be shown, at his first opening of the book, what would be most fitting for him to do. In this he was guided by the spirit of the saints and other men of highest perfection, who, as we read, did the same thing in their longing for sanctity.³

93 He rose from prayer and, in a spirit of humility and with a contrite heart, and fortifying himself with the sign of the holy cross, he took the book from the altar and opened it in fear and trembling. And it happened, when he opened the book,

that the first thing to meet his eye was the passion of Our Lord Jesus Christ, and the passage saying that he would suffer a great ordeal.[4] To avoid any suspicion that this was just coincidence, he opened the book a second and a third time, and found the same passage or a similar passage each time. Then Francis, being filled with the Holy Spirit, knew that it was his lot to enter the kingdom of God through many trials and tribulations and conflicts. But this valiant knight was not disturbed by the wars that threatened, nor dismayed that he was to fight for the Lord in the battlefields of this world. One who had toiled so long, and passed beyond the limits of human strength without yielding even to himself, had no fear of giving way to the foe. In truth, Francis' fervour was extraordinary, and if in ages past there had ever been anyone to equal him in purpose, no one was ever found his superior in aspiration. He knew it was easier for him to achieve perfection in a practical way rather than to talk about it, so it was not into words that he put all his strength and might (for words by themselves do no good) but into holy deeds. So he remained unshaken and happy and sang songs of happiness in his heart to himself and to God. In consequence, he who had been so exultant over the smallest revelation was deemed worthy of a greater, and he who was found trustworthy in a few things, was made ruler over many.[5]

NOTES

1 See Psalm 72.1.
2 2 Corinthians 1.3.
3 St Augustine and St Gregory of Tours, among others, did the same. Bibliomancy, or the random consultation of books to discover prophetic advice, has a very long history.
4 The precise reference is unclear.
5 Matthew 25.21.

Chapter III

The Vision of a Man With the Likeness of a Crucified Seraph

94 Two years before he gave his soul back to heaven, while he was staying in the hermitage called Alverna[1] (so called from the mountain on which it stands), Francis had a vision in which he saw a man like a seraph: he had six wings and was standing above him with his hands outstretched and his feet joined together,

St Francis Receiving the Stigmata

and was fixed to a cross. Two wings were lifted above his head, and two were spread ready for flight, and two covered his whole body. When Francis saw this he was utterly amazed: he could not fathom what this vision might mean. He was overcome with happiness and filled with intense joy at the kindly and gracious way the seraph was looking at him, and the seraph's beauty was indescribable, but the fact that he was nailed to a cross, and the sight of his cruel suffering terrified Francis. Consequently he was both sad and happy, if I can so describe him; joy and grief alternated in him. He wondered anxiously what the vision could possibly represent, and racked his brains trying to make sense of it. But still he could grasp no clear idea of its meaning, and as the strangeness of the vision continued to haunt him, the marks of nails began to appear on his hands and feet just like those he had seen on the crucified figure above him.

95 His hands and feet seemed to be pierced by nails, the heads of the nails appearing on the inside of his hands and the upper side of his feet, and their points protruding on the other side. On the palms of his hands these marks were round, but on the outer side they were longer, and there were little pieces of flesh projecting from the surface which looked like the ends of nails, bent and hammered back. So too there were the marks of nails imprinted on his feet, and the flesh was swollen where the nails appeared. His right side was scarred as if it had been pierced by a spear, and it often seeped blood, so that his tunic and undergarment were frequently drenched in it. Ah, how few were privileged to see the sacred wound in his side while Francis, crucified servant of his crucified Lord, was living! But Brother Elias[2] was fortunate enough to be granted that privilege, and Rufino[3] was no less fortunate, for he touched it with his own hands. It happened when Brother Rufino put his hand under Francis' tunic one day to ease an itch for him, and his hand slipped down to his right side, as can easily happen, and he chanced to touch the precious wound. When he felt Rufino's hand there, Francis was deeply distressed, and he

pushed his hand away and cried out to the Lord to forgive the man. For he was always most careful to conceal his wounds from strangers, and took such pains to hide them even from those close to him that even the Brothers at his side and his most devoted followers for a long time knew nothing about them. And though the servant and friend of the Most High saw that the wounds which covered him were like so many pearls, an adornment of precious jewels, and that he had been singled out to be honoured in a way no other man had ever been, still he never became conceited at heart and never sought to please anyone by revealing his secret for the sake of vainglory. Rather, to prevent worldly adulation from robbing him of the grace he had been given, he did everything he possibly could to keep it hidden.

96 He made it his habit to reveal his great secret to no one or to very few, fearing that if he did reveal it to people, they would tell it to others as proof of the special affection he had for them, and in consequence he might suffer some loss in the grace that had been bestowed on him. So a text which was ever in his heart and often on his lips was: 'Thy words have I hid in mine heart, that I might not sin against thee'.[4] And whenever any lay people came to meet him and he wanted to avoid conversation with them, he had given this text to the Brothers and sons who lived with him as their cue: as soon as he recited the verse, they were courteously to show their guests the door.

He had learnt from experience that it was a bad thing to tell everybody everything, and he knew that no man can be spiritual whose secret virtues are not greater and more perfect than those on the surface that can be judged by the world. Indeed, he had found some people who agreed with him openly but disagreed with him inwardly, who praised him to his face and mocked him behind his back, who won a name for themselves, but made Francis suspicious of 'righteous' folk. For evil often strives to denigrate purity, and because of the lie that is familiar to many the truth spoken by a few is not believed.

1 Alverna, today known as La Verna, is a pine-clad mountain about 20 miles north-north-east of Arezzo in Tuscany. It was given to Francis by Count Orlando of Chiusi in 1213 as a place where he and his friars could go to refresh themselves in prayer and contemplation. High on the mountain there is a famous Franciscan monastery and one can still see (in the Cappella delle Stimmate) the exact spot where Francis received the stigmata in 1224.

2 Brother Elias of Assisi, or of Cortona. After the death of Peter of Catania, Elias was Vicar of the Order until Francis died. He was Minister General in 1232, but was deposed in 1239, and died in 1253.

3 Brother Rufino was a cousin of St Clare. He died in 1270.

4 Psalm 119.11.

Chapter IV

Francis' Religious Fervour, and the Infirmity of his Eyes

97 Throughout this same period of his life Francis began to suffer from a variety of bodily ailments, and these were more serious than anything he had had before. Having utterly mortified his body and brought it under subjection over the course of many years, he now began to suffer frequent infirmities. For 18 years he had given his body little or no rest at all, he had travelled vast distances in any number of regions so that the willing spirit, the devoted spirit, the fervent spirit which lived within him might sow everywhere the seeds of God's word. He filled the whole earth with the gospel of Christ so energetically that often in one day he made his way round four or five villages, or even cities, preaching the kingdom of God in each of them; and edifying all who heard him no less by his example than by his words, he made his whole body speak for him. For in Francis the flesh was so at harmony with the spirit and so obedient to it that while the spirit strove to achieve perfect sanctity, the flesh not only made

no resistance but proved only too ready to run ahead of it. As it is written: 'My soul hath thirsted after thee, in what manifold ways my flesh also!'[1] For his continual subjection of the flesh had made it compliant, and it was by his daily subordination of himself that he had attained such pre-eminence in virtue; for what is habitual often becomes second nature.

98 But because it is nature's law and the way of man's condition that from day to day the outward man must perish, though the inward man is renewed, that most precious vessel in which a heavenly treasure was hidden began to be shaken on every side and to suffer the loss of all its strength. But since 'when a man finishes then he shall begin, and when he stops then shall he work',[2] as his flesh grew weaker his spirit became even more vigorous, for he was so passionate about the salvation of souls and so thirsted for his neighbours' good that when he was no longer able to walk unaided he travelled about the country riding on an ass. The Brothers often warned him about his health and begged him most insistently to allow his sick and feeble frame some sort of respite and to let the doctors help him. But Francis, with that noble spirit of his intent on heaven, and longing only for his bodily dissolution and union with Christ, absolutely refused to do this. But since he had not yet experienced all the sufferings of Christ in his flesh (though he carried his stigmata upon his body), God had even greater mercy on him and he was afflicted by a deadly infirmity of the eyes. As his sickness grew worse from day to day and seemed daily to be aggravated by neglect, at length Brother Elias (whom Francis had chosen to take care of his personal needs, and whom he had made father over the other Brothers[3]) pressed him not to turn his back on medicine, but to receive it in the name of the Son of God, by whom it had been created, and quoted the saying: 'The Most High has created medicine out of the earth and the prudent man will not refuse it.'[4] Francis then had the grace to acquiesce and he humbly followed Elias' advice.

1 Compare Psalm 63.2.
2 Ecclesiasticus 18.6.
3 This alludes to Elias' appointment as Vicar of the Order. See page 98 note 2.
4 Ecclesiasticus 38.4.

◄━━►

Chapter V

The Saint's Reception at Rieti by Hugo Bishop of Ostia; His Prediction that Hugo Would be Bishop of the Whole World

◄━━►

99 But though many came to help him with their medicines no remedy could be found, and Francis went to the city of Rieti where there lived a man who was said to be very successful in his treatment of this disease. When Francis arrived there he was received most kindly and honourably by the whole Roman curia which was then quartered in Rieti.[1] But he was treated with particular respect by Hugo Bishop of Ostia, who was pre-eminent in the papal court for his virtue and holiness of life. Francis had chosen Hugo, with the will and consent of Pope Honorius, as father and lord over all his Brothers and over his whole religious Order, because he loved blessed poverty and had the greatest reverence for holy simplicity. Hugo lived his life as the Brothers did and in his longing for holiness was simple with the simple, humble with the humble, and like a poor man with the poor. He was a Brother among the Brothers, and among the lesser Brothers he was lowliest of all. He strove, so far as it was permitted him, to make himself in his life and conduct just like one of the rest. He was anxious to establish holy religion everywhere, and the noble fame of his even nobler life enlarged the Order greatly in distant parts. The Lord had given him a learned tongue and with it he confounded the adversaries of truth, repelled the enemies of the

cross of Christ, brought sinners back to the true path, made peace between those who were in conflict and bound in a stronger bond of charity those who lived in concord. Bishop Hugo was a 'burning and shining light' in the Church of God, a 'chosen arrow'[2] ready for use in due season. How often he would cast off his costly garments, put on shabby clothing and, going about barefoot like one of the Brothers, perform the duties of peacemaker! This he took pains to do between a man and his neighbour whenever it was necessary; between God and man, always. For this reason, not long after, God singled him out for the highest distinction and chose him as pastor over the whole of his holy Church.

100 And to prove that this choice was inspired by God and brought about through the will of Christ Jesus, Francis predicted it long before: he both foretold it in so many words, and foreshadowed it in his behaviour. For when through the working of God's grace Francis' Order was beginning to expand appreciably and was lifting its crowning glory of merits to heaven like a cedar in God's paradise, and as a choice vine was spreading its sacred branches over the whole breadth of the earth, Francis went to his lordship Pope Honorius, who then ruled the Church, and humbly begged him to appoint Hugo, Bishop of Ostia, as Protector and governor of himself and all his Brothers. The pope granted Francis' prayers and graciously conferred upon Bishop Hugo his own authority over the Order of the Brothers.[3] Hugo accepted it with godly humility and, like a faithful and wise servant set over the Lord's household, he strove in every way he could to administer the food of eternal life to those committed to his charge. So Francis bowed to his will in everything, and he revered him and regarded him with the greatest respect and affection. He was led by the Holy Spirit, which filled his whole being, so he could see clearly far in advance what the eyes of the world were to witness afterwards. For instance, whenever he wrote to Hugo on some matter concerning his Order, or rather because he was impelled

to do so by the great love he felt for him, he could never bring himself to address him as 'Bishop of Ostia' or 'of Velletri',[4] the usual titles by which others addressed him, but, after deciding on the subject of his letter, he would begin it 'To the Most Reverend Father', or 'To the Lord Hugo, Bishop of All the World'. And often he would greet him with the most fervent blessings and, though he was like a son in his humble deference to him, when the spirit so moved him he would sometimes comfort Hugo in fatherly style so as to strengthen in him 'the blessings of his fathers, until the desire of the everlasting hills should come'.[5]

101 Bishop Hugo returned Francis' love with equal intensity, and so whatever the saint said or did found favour with him, and often he was stirred to the depths by the mere sight of him. He himself bears witness that no matter how disturbed or distressed he might be, when he saw Francis and talked with him, every cloud on the horizon dispersed and his world was at peace again, his cares were banished and joy breathed on him from above.

Hugo ministered to Francis as a servant to his master and whenever he saw him, showed him the reverence due to one of Christ's apostles. Both inwardly and outwardly he did him obeisance, and would often kiss his hands with his consecrated lips. He was most anxious that Francis should recover his eyesight and did all he could to help him, because he knew that a holy and righteous man like him was both necessary and valuable to the Church of God. He felt great sympathy for the whole community of Brothers on account of Francis, and because of the father he pitied the sons. Accordingly he told Francis to take care of himself and not to reject the things needed to treat his illness, warning him that his neglect of these things might be considered more of a sin than a virtue. And Francis humbly listened to what this most respected lord and beloved father told him, and thereafter he did all that was needful to treat his infirmity with greater care and more peace of mind. But by now the disease had worsened to such an extent that the most skilful medical advice and most drastic remedies were imperative if his condition was to improve at all. So his head was cauterized in several places, his veins were bled, his eyes were covered with plasters and washed with eye salves: but he made no progress, and in fact almost every day was getting worse.

NOTES

1 The curia was in Rieti from June 1225 to the end of January 1226.
2 See John 5.35 and compare Isaiah 49.2.
3 This happened earlier, perhaps as early as 1216, and was confirmed later by Honorius III in 1220 or 1221.
4 Hugo was Bishop of Ostia, at the mouth of the Tiber, and also of Velletri, which is inland about 30 miles south-south-east.
5 Compare Genesis 49.26.

Chapter VI

The Conduct of the Brothers Who Looked After Francis; His Plans at This Time

102 All this Francis bore for about two years with absolute patience and humility, giving thanks to God in all things. But in order to concentrate his mind wholly on God, to spend his time in ecstatic contemplation of the bliss of heaven and to present himself on high in the fulness of grace before the most gracious and serene Lord of all, he had entrusted himself to the care of certain of the Brothers who had earned his especial love.

For these were men of virtue, devoted to God, pleasing to the saints, acceptable to men, and Francis leaned upon them like a house on its four columns. For the present, I suppress their names out of respect for their modesty (which is a close friend to them, since they are spiritual men). Modesty is an ornament of all ages, the witness to innocence, the mark of a virtuous mind, the rod of correction, the special glory of the conscience, the guardian of reputation, and the banner of all righteousness. All these Brothers were pre-eminent for their modesty, and it made them loveable and kindly to their fellow men; it was a grace they all possessed in common, but each of them was graced by his own special virtue. One[1] was famed for his exceptional discretion, another[2] for his extraordinary patience, another for his outstanding simplicity,[3] and the last[4] combined robustness of physique with gentleness of character. These Brothers tried with the utmost vigilance and zeal and with all their will to secure their blessed father's peace of mind, and cared for his bodily infirmity, refusing no hardship or toil in their eagerness to devote themselves entirely to serving the saint.

103 But though Francis had been brought to perfection of grace before God, and shone among the men of this world for his good works, he was still for ever thinking of beginning new works of even greater perfection, and, like a veteran in God's camp, itching to challenge the foe and stir up war afresh. He meant, with Christ as his captain, to do great things, and though his limbs were failing and his body was all but dead, he hoped to triumph over the enemy in a fresh struggle. For true virtue knows no limit of time, since the expectation of a reward is eternal. So Francis was on fire with an intense longing to return to the first beginnings of humility, and rejoicing in hope because of his boundless love, he planned to reduce his body (even though by now it was on the brink of collapse) to its former state of subjection. He removed from himself completely any cares that might impede him, and totally silenced the clamour of all anxieties. And when because of his infirmity he was forced to moderate his former rigour, he would say: 'Let us begin to serve the Lord God, Brothers, because up to now we have made little or no progress.' He did not think he had yet attained the goal he yearned for, and persisting tirelessly in his quest to attain new holiness of life, he hoped always to make a start. He wanted to return to the service of lepers again, and to be despised by the world as he had once been. He determined to shun human companionship

and withdraw to the most remote places, so that once he had rid himself of all cares and cast aside all anxiety for others, the only thing standing between him and God would be the wall of the flesh.

104 For he saw many people chasing after positions of power, men whose temerity he hated, and whom he was striving to cure of this madness by his example. He used to say it was a good thing and acceptable in God's eyes to take care of others, but that the only men fit to undertake the care of souls were those who would seek in it no personal satisfaction, but would always attend to the will of God in all things; men, namely, who would put nothing before their own salvation, and paid no heed to the approval of those in their care, but only to their advancement, aiming not at self-display before men, but glory before God; men who did not strive for preferment, but were afraid of it; who, when it came their way, were not made arrogant but were humbled, and when it was taken from them were not disheartened, but overjoyed. He said it was dangerous to be in authority, especially at that time, when wickedness had grown to such an extent, and evil was rife; indeed he declared it was better to be ruled by others. He was saddened that some had abandoned their earlier way of life and embraced new ideas and forgotten their former simplicity; accordingly he felt deep sorrow that men who had once been wholly intent upon higher things had stooped to what was base and worthless, and had abandoned true joys to roam and wander in frivolity and folly about the field of an empty freedom. So he asked that God's mercy might save his sons from this error, and prayed most earnestly that they might be kept in the grace that had been given them.[5]

NOTES

1 This is generally taken to mean Brother Angelo Tancredi.
2 Probably Brother Rufino.
3 Probably Brother Leo, father confessor and secretary of Francis.

4 Probably Brother John de Laudibus (of Lodi) who touched Francis'
stigmata while the saint was still alive.

5 Compare Romans 12.3.

Chapter VII

How Francis Went from Siena to Assisi;
of the Church of St Mary of the Portiuncula
and the Blessing He Gave the Brothers

---

105 But in the sixth month before his death, when Francis was in Siena having his eyes treated, he began to be seriously ill all over the rest of his body. His stomach had been weakened by a chronic illness and liver malfunction, and he vomited so much blood that he appeared to be at death's door. Brother Elias was some way away when he heard the news, but he came to him as quickly as he could; and upon his arrival Francis made such a quick recovery that he was able to leave Siena and go with Elias to Le Celle[1] near Cortona. Francis remained there some time, during which his stomach swelled, his legs and feet puffed up, and his stomach condition steadily deteriorated to a point where he could scarcely take any food. He then asked Brother Elias to have him taken to Assisi and Elias, loyal son, did as his kind father asked, and when everything was ready, he took him to the place he longed for.

At the saint's arrival the whole city celebrated and the praise of God was on everyone's lips. The reason for their great joy was that they were hoping, each and every one of them, that the holy man would soon die in their midst.[2]

106 And so, by the will of God, it happened that his holy soul was released from the flesh and passed to the kingdom of heaven at the very place where, when he was still in the flesh, he was first given knowledge of things above and the saving unction was poured upon him.[3] For though he knew that

106

the kingdom of heaven was established in every place upon earth and believed that divine grace was given to the chosen of God no matter where, he had discovered from experience that the Church of St Mary of the Portiuncula was filled with richer grace than anywhere else and was visited by heavenly spirits.[4] So he used often to say to the Brothers:

My sons, see that you never leave this place. If you are driven out through one door, come back through the other. For this place is truly holy, it is the dwelling-place of God. Here when we were few, the Most High made our numbers grow. Here he enlightened the hearts of his poor followers with the light of his wisdom. Here he set our hearts aflame with the fire of his love. Here he who prays with a sincere heart will have what he asks for, and he who offends will be punished more severely. So, my sons, count this dwelling-place of God worthy of all honour: here give thanks to God with all your heart and with the voice of joy and praise.

107 Meanwhile, as his sickness grew, all his bodily strength failed, and he was so weak he could not move at all. And when one of the Brothers asked him what he would rather suffer – this long, lingering sickness, or some cruel martyrdom at the hands of an executioner – he replied:

My son, whatever the Lord my God wishes to do to me or to do with me, that is and has always been dearest and sweetest and most acceptable to me, for I desire always to be found responsive and obedient to his will in all things. Yet I could bear any sort of martyrdom rather than even three days of this sickness, and I do not refer to the reward of martyrdom, only to the degree of suffering it causes.

. . . In fact not a single part of his body was now free from the cruellest pain, and as the warmth of life gradually left him, he was daily drawing nearer to the end. His doctors were amazed, the Brothers astonished that his spirit could live on in flesh so dead, for the flesh had all gone and nothing but skin clung to his bones.

108 Now when Francis saw that his last day was fast approaching (and this had been made known to him two years before by divine revelation[5]) he called those of the Brothers he wished to see, and, as it was given him from above, he blessed each one, just as of old Jacob[6] blessed his sons, or rather like a second Moses[7] who, when he was about to climb the mountain appointed by God, showered his blessings upon each of the tribes of Israel.

When Brother Elias was seated on his left and the other Brothers were sitting round him, Francis reached across and placed his right hand on Elias' head, and since he had lost all sight in his bodily eyes, asked: 'Who is this?' 'Elias,' they told him. 'And this is my wish', he said.

First, my son, I bless you yourself above all things and in all things.[8] And just as the Most High has multiplied my Brothers and sons in your hands, so also I bless them all through you and by my blessing upon you. May God, King of all, bless you in heaven and on earth. I bless you with all the blessings I can give and more, and what I cannot do for you may he do who can do all things. May God remember our work and toil and may a portion be reserved for you in the reward of the just. May you meet with every blessing you desire, and may all you ask worthily be granted. Farewell, all my sons, in the fear of God: remain in him always, for a very great trial is to come upon you and trouble is at hand. Happy are those who persevere as they have begun, for the scandals that are coming will cause some to leave the Brotherhood. I am hastening to the Lord, and go in all confidence to my God, whom I have served in my heart with devotion.

Francis had at the time been staying in the palace of the Bishop of Assisi, so he asked his Brothers to carry him as quickly as possible to the convent at St Mary of the Portiuncula. For he wished to give back his soul to God at the very spot where, as has been said, he first fully knew the way of truth.

1 Le Celle was a couple of miles north of Cortona, which is about 40 miles north-west of Assisi. It was one of the first friaries or convents of the Brotherhood.
2 The citizens of Assisi were anxious to keep the saint's remains in Assisi. (Their rivals the Perugians later tried unsuccessfully to steal the body from its resting place in St George's.)
3 That is, he was 'saved' on hearing the Gospel reading on the feast of St Matthias, probably in 1208.
4 *Second Life* c.19 (end): 'Francis used to say that it had been revealed to him by God that the Blessed Mother loved this church ... with a special love.'
5 See Paragraph 109 below.
6 Genesis 49.1–27.
7 Deuteronomy 33.1ff.
8 An echo of Ephesians 4.6 where God is described as 'above all and through all and in all'.

Chapter VIII

What Francis Did and Said at the Time of his Holy Death

109 A space of 20 years had now passed since his conversion, exactly as had been made known to him by the will of God. For once when Francis and Brother Elias were staying at Foligno, one night when they were asleep a priest dressed in white, a man of great age and venerable appearance, stood before Elias and said: 'Up you get, Brother, and tell Brother Francis that eighteen years have passed since he renounced the world and gave himself to Christ, and that he will remain in this life only two more years, and then the Lord will call him to himself and he will go the way of all flesh.' And so it happened that the Lord's word declared long before was now fulfilled at the appointed time.

When therefore Francis had rested a few days in the place where he had so longed to be, and knew that the time of his death was imminent, he summoned two of his Brothers who were his spiritual sons,[1] and told them to sing praises to the Lord for his approaching death – or rather, for the new life that was at hand – and to sing them loudly and joyfully. Then Francis suddenly began with all the strength he could muster to recite the psalm of David which begins: 'I cried unto the Lord with my voice, with my voice unto the Lord did I make my supplication'.[2] But one of the Brothers who was standing there, a Brother whom Francis loved particularly, seeing how things were, and realizing the end was near, in his great anxiety for all the Brothers said to him: 'Alas, kind father, your sons are now without a father, they are robbed of the true light of their eyes! Remember the orphans you are leaving and forgive them all their faults and cheer them all, those present and those absent, with your holy blessing.' Francis replied: 'See, my son, God calls me to him. I forgive all the offences and faults of my Brothers, absent and present, and, so far as in me lies, I absolve them. Tell them this and bless them all for me.'

110 Francis then ordered the book of the Gospels to be brought and asked that the Gospel according to John should be read to him, beginning at the verse: 'Six days before the Passover, Jesus, knowing that the hour was come that he should pass from this world to his father'.[3] Elias in fact had intended to read this Gospel to him before he was told to do so; also this was the very place where the book had fallen open earlier, though the volume from which the Gospel was to be read was a complete text of the whole Bible. Francis then ordered that he be clothed in a hair shirt and strewn with ashes, since he was soon to become dust and ashes. At this all the Brothers gathered around their father and leader, and as they stood reverently at his side awaiting his blessed death and happy end, Francis' most holy soul was released from the flesh and immersed in the abyss of light, and his body fell asleep in the Lord. And one of his Brothers and disciples (a man well known, but whose name I feel I must withhold here because, while he is still alive, he has no wish to boast of the fact[4]) saw the holy father's soul rise over many waters straight to heaven. It was

like a star, yet somehow as big as the moon and as brilliant as the sun and borne aloft on a small white cloud.

111 So I cannot refrain from crying:

O how glorious a saint was this, whose soul his disciple saw ascend into heaven, fair as the moon, choice as the sun, and as he rose upon the white cloud, he gleamed most gloriously! Truly you are a light of the world, shining in the Church of Christ more brightly than the sun! See, you have now withdrawn your rays and, retired to the kingdom of light, you have exchanged the company of us wretched creatures for the company of angels and saints! O kindest father of glorious renown, do not cast aside your care for your sons, though you have now cast aside the flesh that was like theirs. You know, indeed you know, in what a perilous state you have left them, for it was your happy presence alone that always mercifully relieved their countless trials and frequent anxieties. O most holy, most merciful father, you were always ready to take pity on your sinful sons and kindly forgive them! For this we bless you, worthy father, whom the Most High has blessed, who is ever God, blessed above all things. Amen.

NOTES

1 According to tradition these were Brother Angelo Tancredi and Brother Leo.
2 Psalm 142.1.
3 A conflation of John 12.1 and 13.1.
4 According to one source this was Brother James of Assisi.

———

Chapter IX

The Grief of the Brothers, and Their Joy When They Saw His Stigmata; the Wings of the Seraphim

———

112 At the news large crowds of people gathered praising God and saying: 'Glory and blessings be upon you, O

Lord God, for entrusting to our unworthy keeping so precious a jewel! Praise and glory be to you, ineffable Trinity!' The whole city of Assisi rushed there in crowds, and the entire region hurried to see the wonderful things God had manifested so gloriously in his saintly servant. Each one, as his heartfelt joy prompted him, sang a hymn of gladness, and everyone blessed the Saviour's omnipotence for the granting of their desire.

Francis' sons were filled with grief at the loss of so great a father, and showed their dutiful affection with tears and sighs. But their sorrow was tempered by an unbelievable joy, and a miracle happened which utterly stunned them. Their mourning was turned to song, and their weeping to jubilation.

Never had they heard or read in the Scriptures of what now appeared before their very eyes: indeed, they could hardly have been persuaded to believe what they were seeing if the evidence had not been so clear and irrefutable. For there on his body, indisputably, appeared the form of the cross and passion of the spotless Lamb who washed away the sins of the world. It was as if he had only lately been taken down from the cross; his hands and his feet seemed pierced by nails and his right side wounded by a spear. They saw his flesh, which had been dark before, gleaming with a brilliant whiteness and by reason of its beauty giving assurance of the rewards of a blessed resurrection. Finally they saw that his face was like the face of an angel; it was as if he were alive, and not dead; and the rest of his body had become as soft and supple as that of a young child. His sinews were not contracted as those of dead people usually are, and his skin had not hardened; his limbs were not rigid, but could be turned at will this way and that.

113 And while he shone with such miraculous beauty before the gaze of the Brothers, and his flesh had become even more white, it was wonderful to see, in his hands and feet, not in fact the holes made by the nails, but the nails them-selves[1] formed out of his flesh and still retaining the blackness of

iron, and his right side red with blood. These signs of his martyrdom, so far from filling the minds of those who looked on them
with revulsion, lent his body great beauty and grace, as little black
stones do when inset in a white pavement.

His Brothers and sons pushed forward to see, and weeping they
kissed the hands and feet of the loving father who was leaving
them, kissed his right side, too, where the spear wound presented a
solemn memorial of the one who, in pouring forth blood and water
from that same place, reconciled the world to his Father. Anyone
who was permitted to kiss, or indeed just to see, the sacred stigmata of Jesus Christ which Francis bore on his body, thought he
was being granted a unique privilege. For who at this sight would
feel moved to weep rather than to be glad? Or if he wept, would
it not be for joy rather than for sorrow? Whose breast so iron-like
that it would not be moved to sighing? Whose heart so stony that
it would not burst with compunction, not be fired with love of
God, not be inspired to acts of good will? Who could be so dull,
so unfeeling as not to grasp the obvious truth that, as Francis was
honoured on earth by such a matchless gift, so he is magnified in
heaven by an indescribable glory?

114 Such a matchless gift and proof of such special love,
that a soldier should be adorned with the same glorious arms that, in their surpassing majesty, were fit for the king
alone! O miracle worthy of everlasting memory, O sacrament
worthy of undying wonder and awe, which to the eye of faith
betokens that mystery in which the blood of the spotless Lamb
flowing copiously through five outlets washed away the sins of the
world! O the sublime splendour of the quickening cross that gives
life to the dead, whose burden presses so lightly and gives so sweet
a pain that through it the dead flesh lives and the feeble spirit is
made strong! How much he loved you and how gloriously you
adorned him! Glory and blessing be to God only wise, who works
new signs and new wonders to comfort the minds of the weak by
new revelations, so that by means of visible miracles their hearts

may be drawn to a love of things invisible! O how wondrous and admirable God's plan: for, so that there should be no doubts concerning this new miracle, he mercifully first revealed in a heavenly being what he was soon after to do miraculously to one living on earth. And indeed the true Father of mercies wanted to show how great a reward was merited by one who strove to love him with all his heart, the reward, namely, of a place in the highest order of celestial spirits, a place nearest to himself.[2]

And we can without doubt win this reward if we, like the seraphim, extend two wings above our head, that is if, following the example of St Francis, we keep our intentions pure and our actions upright in all our works, and if we offer these up to God and strive tirelessly to please him alone in everything. Now these wings must necessarily be joined to cover the head, because the Father of Light will by no means accept the uprightness of a deed without purity of intention, nor the converse, for as he himself says: 'If thine eye be single, thy whole body shall be full of light. But if it be evil, thy whole body shall be full of darkness'.[3] For no eye is whole that does not see what it should see, because it lacks knowledge of the truth; nor is that which looks at what it should not look at, because its intention is not pure. In the first case plain reason will conclude that the eye was not whole, but blind; in the second the eye is evil. The feathers of these wings are the love of the Father, the merciful Saviour, and fear of the Lord, the terrible judge; and these feathers must raise the souls of the elect from earthly things by curbing evil inclinations and ordering the affections in charity. We should also fly upon two wings to show charity to our neighbour in two ways: by refreshing his soul with the word of God and nourishing his body with earthly sustenance. But these two wings are very rarely joined together, because scarcely anyone can fulfil both these obligations. The feathers of these wings are the different works we must perform for our neighbour in order to advise and help him. Lastly, it is with these two wings that the body, which is unadorned by merits, must be covered, and this is correctly done when, after it is stripped bare

114

by the intrusion of sin, it is reclothed in innocence by means of contrition and confession. The feathers of these wings are the manifold affections which are engendered by hatred of sin and hunger for justice.

115 All these things were done to perfection by the blessed father Francis, who bore the image and form of a seraph, and persevered upon the cross until he was deemed worthy to rise to the ranks of the spirits above. For he was always on the cross, shunning no hardship or pain if only he could accomplish the will of the Lord in all he did and suffered. Moreover, the Brothers who lived with him knew how constantly every day his talk was of Jesus, how sweetly and tenderly he spoke, how kind and loving the things he said to them. His words issued from the welling over of his heart, it was the bubbling forth of the spring of enlightened love that filled all his inward being. Indeed he was constantly with Jesus; he bore Jesus always in his heart, Jesus on his lips, Jesus in his ears, Jesus in his eyes, Jesus in his hands, Jesus in every other part of his being. How often, when he sat down to eat, and thought of Jesus, or heard or spoke his name, he forgot bodily food and, as has been written of another saint: 'Seeing he did not see and hearing he did not hear'.[4] What is more, very often while he was walking along meditating on Jesus, or singing of him, he would forget where he was going and call upon all the elements to praise him. And because of the wonderful love with which he always bore and jealously guarded 'Christ Jesus and him crucified'[5] in his heart, he was singled out to be marked in a most glorious way with the sign of him whom in ecstasy of mind he contemplated sitting in indescribable and incomprehensible glory at the right hand of the Father, with whom he lives and reigns, triumphs and governs in unity with the Holy Spirit, God eternally glorious throughout all ages. Amen.

NOTES

1 Celano and, later, Bonaventure base their description of the stigmata

on that of Brother Elias, an eye witness, contained in a letter he wrote to Gregory of Naples (Minister General in France) to tell him about Francis' death. But Elias' Latin is ambiguous, and is capable of meaning no more than that the holes in Francis' hands and feet were blackened and seemed to have been made by nails.

2 That is, the order of seraphim.

3 Matthew 6.22–3.

4 This was written of St Bernard (d. 1153), the Cistercian monk and Abbot of Clairvaux.

5 1 Corinthians 2.2.

———

Chapter X

The Grief of the Ladies at St Damian's; and How Francis Was Buried with Praise and Glory

———

116 Francis' Brothers and sons, who had gathered with huge crowds of people from the neighbouring towns, were overjoyed to be present at such a great solemnity, and spent the whole of the night on which the holy father had died singing the praises of God, and so sweet was the sound of their jubilation and the brightness of their tapers that it seemed the angels themselves were keeping vigil. And when morning came the people of Assisi gathered with all the clergy and took Francis' sacred body from the place where he had died, and with hymns of praise and the sounding of trumpets, carried it in great reverence into the city. They all took branches of olive and other trees and performed the sacred obsequies with solemnity, and lit by a myriad torches they loudly performed their offices of praise. With the sons carrying their father and the flock following their shepherd, who was hastening to meet the Shepherd of all, they reached the place where he had himself first established the religious order of holy virgins and poor ladies,[1] and they placed him in the church of St Damian, where these daughters lived whom he had won for the Lord. Then

the little window was opened through which at the appointed time the handmaids of Christ used to receive the sacrament of the Lord's body. The coffin also, with its treasure of celestial virtues, was opened, the coffin in which the saint who used to bear so many was borne by a few.[2] And suddenly Lady Clare arrived with her daughters to see the father who would never speak to them or return to them again, but was hastening elsewhere; Clare, illustrious[3] for her holy virtues, who was the first mother and indeed the first member of this holy order.

The Burial Rites of St Francis

117 As they gazed upon him they redoubled their sighs, and weeping copiously and with heartfelt groans they began to cry softly:

Father, father, what shall we do? Why are you forsaking your poor daughters? To whom can we turn now? Why did you not send us rejoicing before you where you are going, instead of leaving us here in our misery? What do you bid us do, shut up here in this prison, now you will never again visit us as you used to? With you all our comfort is gone, and buried to the world as we are no such solace is left us. Who will comfort us in such great poverty, for we are as poor in merit as in material things? O father of the poor, lover of poverty! Who shall help us in temptation? You knew so many temptations and knew how to overcome them. Who shall comfort us now in times of trouble? You always helped us in all the troubles that so beset us. Ah, how bitter this parting, how cruel our loss! O how dreadful this death, slaying thousands of sons and daughters by bereaving them of their great father, and hastening to remove beyond recall the one who more than any other caused our feeble efforts to prosper!

But virginal modesty kept them from weeping overmuch, and it was out of place to weep excessively for one at whose passing the angelic host thronged together, and the citizens of heaven and the saints and all God's household were exultant. So, torn between sorrow and joy, they kissed his radiant hands, hands that were adorned with the most precious gems and glittering pearls.[4] And when his body was removed, the door was closed which will surely never again be opened to sorrow so great. Ah, how bitterly everyone grieved at the wretched and pitiful wailing of the sisters! Loudest of all were the lamentations of his sorrowful sons; yet their special grief was shared by all: hardly anyone could refrain from weeping, when the angels of peace themselves wept so bitterly.

118 Finally, when they had all reached the city they laid his most holy body amid great rejoicing and exultation in

a sacred place[5] (a place henceforth more sacred still), where to the glory of the supreme, Almighty God, Francis gives spiritual enlightenment to the world with a succession of new miracles, just as before his death he had wonderfully enlightened it with all he taught in his holy preaching. Thanks be to God. Amen.

There, most holy and blessed father: I have given you the praises that are due to you and of which you are worthy, though they are insufficient, and I have written a narrative, such as it is, of your deeds. Grant me in return, therefore, wretch that I am, that I may so worthily follow you in this life that I may deserve to meet you in the next. Remember, gracious father, your poor sons, to whom hardly any comfort is left now you, their one and only solace, are gone! For though you, the first and greatest of their number, are now with the choirs of angels and seated among the apostles on a throne of glory, they still lie in the filth of the mire, shut up in a dark prison, crying sorrowfully to you: 'Father, present to Jesus Christ, Son of the Most High Father, his sacred wounds, and show him the mark of the cross in your side, feet and hands, that he may in his mercy deign to show his own wounds to the Father, who for this will surely look favourably on us in our misery. Amen.' So be it. So be it.

NOTES

1 That is, the Portiuncula.
2 Perhaps an allusion to Isaiah 46.4.
3 Another play on Clare's name. See Part I Chapter VIII note 3.
4 Celano is referring to the stigmata.
5 Francis was first buried in the church of St George, Assisi. Then in 1230, when the basilica had been built in his honour, his remains were taken there.

Here Ends Part II

PART III

Here Begins Part III:
The Canonization of Our Blessed Father
Francis and His Miracles

Chapter I

$\overset{\frown}{}$

119 So our illustrious father Francis brought an auspicious beginning to an even more auspicious end, and in the twentieth year of his conversion most auspiciously commended his spirit to heaven, where crowned with glory and honour and having gained a place amid stones of fire[1] he stands at the throne of God, and is engaged in furthering the interests of those he has left on earth. What indeed could be denied one in the marks of whose sacred stigmata can be seen the form of him who, being equal to the Father, 'sits at the right hand of the Majesty on High, the brightness of his glory and the express image of his substance',[2] and purges the sins of mankind? How could he not be heard, when he has been 'made conformable unto the death of Jesus Christ in the fellowship of his suffering',[3] and shows the sacred wounds in his hands and feet and side?

Francis is indeed already cheering and gladdening the whole world with new joy, and offering to everyone the blessings of true salvation. He is irradiating the whole world with the brilliant light of his miracles and brightening the whole earth with the radiance of a real star. At the time, the world mourned when deprived of his presence, and at his setting saw itself submerged, as it were, in an abyss of darkness. But now, lit up as at noon with more radiant beams by the rising of this new light, it feels that the darkness everywhere has gone. All its complaining – blessed be God – has now ceased, since every day and in every corner it is filled through him so abundantly with new joy at the plentiful harvest of his holy virtues. From the east and from the west, from the south and from the north, people come who have been aided by his intercession, providing incontestable evidence of the truth of what I have written. Indeed, while he lived in the flesh, Francis loved the things of heaven so exclusively, and refused absolutely to own any property precisely so that he might the more fully and more happily possess the universal good. And so it happened that what he refused in part, he gained in its entirety, and exchanged time for eternity. Everywhere he is helping everyone, everywhere he is close at hand to everyone; and, a true lover of unity, he knows no loss through division.[4]

120 While he yet lived among sinners, Francis roamed the whole world preaching. Now reigning with the angels in heaven above he flies swifter than thought as messenger of the Most High King and bestows bounteous gifts upon all peoples. Accordingly the whole world honours him, reveres him, glorifies him and sings his praises. In truth, everyone shares in the common good.

Who could tell, who could number all the great miracles God is everywhere deigning to work through him? How many miracles indeed Francis is performing in France alone where the king[5] and queen and all the nobles run to kiss and honour the pillow Francis used on his sickbed! France, where all the wise and most learned men (of whom Paris always produces a greater abundance than anywhere else in the world) humbly and most devoutly venerate, admire and honour Francis, an uneducated man and the friend of true sincerity and absolute simplicity. Francis was indeed well named: for he had the frankest[6] and noblest heart in the world.

Those who have experienced his generosity of spirit know how free, how liberal he was in every way, how assured and fearless in all things, with what great strength and spiritual fervour he trampled all worldly things underfoot. And what am I to say about the rest of the world, where diseases are cured and sicknesses banished merely by contact with his girdle, and huge numbers of men and women are delivered from their misfortunes merely by invoking his name?

121 At his tomb, too, new miracles are constantly occurring, and as the number of petitions increases, great blessings

are won there for both body and soul. Sight is restored to the blind, hearing to the deaf, the lame walk again, the dumb speak, people with gout dance for joy, lepers are healed, those with dropsy gain relief, and people suffering from a wide variety of other diseases find themselves cured. Francis' dead body, in fact, is healing living bodies, just as his living body raised dead souls to life again.

The pope, highest of all pontiffs, the leader of Christendom and Vicar of Christ heard all this and understood its importance. He was glad, he was delighted, he was exultant, he was beside himself with joy when he saw the revival of God's Church in his own day by these new mysteries that were like the miracles of old, and he was delighted that it should come about through his own son, the spiritual son whom he had fathered, fostered, cherished in his sacred bosom and nurtured with the food of salvation. The other prelates of the Church also heard the news, the shepherds of the flock, the defenders of the faith, the friends of the Bridegroom[7] who stand at the pope's side, those 'hinges'[8] of the world, the venerable cardinals. They rejoiced for the Church, they shared the pope's joy, and they glorified the Saviour, who with supreme and ineffable wisdom, with supreme and immeasurable goodness, and with supreme and incomprehensible grace chooses the foolish and lowly things of the world in order to draw the mighty to himself. The whole world heard and applauded, and the whole of Catholic Christendom was overwhelmed with joy and was cheered and strengthened beyond measure.

122 But meanwhile there came a sudden change in the world and a new emergency arose. At once the pleasures of peace were disrupted, the torch of envy was lit, and the Church was torn apart by domestic and civil war. The Romans, a rebellious and fierce race of men, vented their fury against their neighbours (as they had often done) and rashly stretched forth their hands against the holy places.[9] The noble Pope Gregory did all he could to stem the tide of wickedness, to curb their savagery, to restrain their violence, and like a buttressed tower he protected

the Church of Christ. Many were the perils that beset her, the havoc increased, and in the rest of the world sinners showed a brazen defiance of God. Using his vast experience to gauge the outcome and weighing up the present situation, Pope Gregory abandoned the city[10] to the rebels in order to deliver the world from rebellions and keep it safe. He went to Rieti,[11] where he was received with due honour; then he proceeded to Spoleto[12] and was shown great respect by all. He stayed there a few days and after putting the affairs of the Church in order, paid a gracious visit with the venerable cardinals to the handmaids of Christ, who were dead and buried to the world in their convent nearby.[13] The holy life and utter poverty of these ladies and their celebrated way of life moved him and everyone else to tears, urged them to despise the world, and kindled in them a longing for the cloistered life . . .

123 Then he hurried on to Assisi[14] where the glorious treasure lay awaiting him, hoping by this to dispel the universal suffering and divert the imminent crisis. At his arrival the whole region was jubilant, the city was filled with exultation, a vast crowd of people celebrated their great joy, and a day already bright was made brighter still by the arrival of new luminaries. Everyone went out to meet him and a solemn vigil was kept. The holy fraternity of Poor Brothers went out to meet him and they all sang sweet songs to Christ the Lord. As soon as the Vicar of Christ reached the place, he went to Francis' sepulchre and greeted it with eager reverence. He sighed repeatedly, he struck his breast, he wept and bowed his venerable head in deep devotion. While he was in Assisi a solemn conference was held to consider the canonization of Francis and the noble assembly of cardinals was often convened to discuss the matter. Many people came there from different parts whose lives had been saved by the holy man: a dazzling number of miracles was attested everywhere, and these were admitted, approved, verified, considered and accepted.

But meanwhile the pope's official business was pressing, and a fresh emergency loomed: the pope moved on to Perugia, from where he meant, with excessive and singular goodness, to return again to Assisi to attend to this vital matter. There followed another council at Perugia, and a sacred assembly of cardinals was held in the private rooms of the lord pope to consider the matter. They were all of one mind and expressed total agreement. An account of the miracles was read out which the cardinals received with great reverence, and they acclaimed the life and conduct of the blessed father and heaped praises upon him.

124 'There is no need of miracles,' they said, 'to attest the holy life of such a holy man. We have seen it with our eyes, handled it with our hands[15] and proved it in the school of truth.' They were all beside themselves for joy, they celebrated, they wept with happiness, and indeed in those tears there was great blessing. At once they fixed the happy day on which they were to fill the whole world with spiritual joy. The solemn day came, a day to be honoured by all ages to come, a day that bathed in rapture sublime not only the dwellings on earth, but even those in heaven. Bishops assembled, abbots came, prelates of the Church arrived from the remotest parts; a king, too, was present,[16] and a splendid throng of counts and princes. All these acted as the pope's escort and with him they entered the city in glorious majesty. They came to the place[17] which had been made ready for the solemn occasion, and the whole company of cardinals, bishops and abbots gathered round the pope. A most distinguished throng of priests and clerics was present; also a blessed and holy company of religious; there too in their modest habits were those who had taken the veil; and a great crowd of people, an almost countless host of men and women. They hurried there from every quarter, people of all ages, the lowly and the great were present, servants and freemen alike.

125 There stood the supreme pontiff, the spouse of the Church of Christ, with all his many sons about him, and a crown of glory on his head in token of his sanctity. He stood there adorned with the pontifical insignia and clad in holy vestments fastened with gold and embellished with precious gemstones. The anointed of the Lord stood there a magnificent and glorious figure in his golden vestments, covered with graven jewels that sparkled with all the lustre of spring, and everyone's gaze was drawn to him. Cardinals and bishops surrounded him, adorned with their gleaming necklaces and wearing garments of brilliant, snowy white, they displayed a beauty more than heavenly, they manifested the joy of the glorified.

Everyone there was awaiting the joyous announcement, the happy news, the honey-sweet words, words of praise that would confer perpetual blessing. First Pope Gregory preached to the whole assembly and in mellifluous and sonorous tones he proclaimed God's praises. He also gave a most noble eulogy in praise of Francis, and as he recounted and described the purity of his life he was in floods of tears. The text of his sermon was: 'He shone in his days as the morning star through clouds or as the moon at the full; and as the shining sun so did he shine in the temple of God'.[18] And when the sermon was ended (a faithful sermon, and worthy of all acceptance[19]) one of the pope's subdeacons, a man named Ottaviano[20] read out before everyone, in ringing tones, a list of the saint's miracles, and Monsignor Riniero,[21] a cardinal-deacon, a man of the keenest intellect and renowned for the piety of his life, expatiated on them most movingly and wept as he spoke. The shepherd of the Church was moved to the depths of his being; he heaved deep sighs, sobbed repeatedly, and streams of tears ran down his cheeks. All the other prelates of the Church were also in floods of tears, and their sacred vestments were wet with their weeping. All the people, too, were in tears, and wearied with waiting for the longed-for moment.

126 Then the pope, lifting his hands to heaven, loudly proclaimed:

To the praise and glory of Almighty God, Father, Son and Holy

Ghost, and of the glorious Virgin Mary, and of the blessed apostles Peter and Paul, and to the honour of the glorious Church of Rome, on the advice of our brothers and the other prelates, we decree that Francis, whom the Lord has glorified in heaven, and whom we venerate on earth, shall be numbered in the catalogue of saints and that his feast day shall be celebrated on the day of his death.

At this announcement the venerable cardinals together with the pope began loudly to chant the *Te Deum*. Then a shout went up, the sound of vast numbers praising God; and the earth re-echoed their deafening voices, the air was filled with their jubilation, and the ground was wet with their tears. New songs were sung[22] and the servants of God expressed their rapture in harmony of spirit. The sweet tones of organs could be heard, and melodious renderings of hymns and psalms. There was the most ravishing fragrance in the air, and the sweetest music that moved all who heard it. The day was radiant indeed, and made brighter still by rays of unusual splendour: people had brought olive branches with them and fresh fronds of other greenery; everyone was dressed in festive attire of gayest colours, and the blessing of peace filled all their hearts with joy. The happy Pope Gregory finally rose from his lofty throne, went down the steps and entered the sanctuary to offer the holy sacrifice of Mass. There with happy lips he kissed the tomb containing the body which was sacred and consecrated to God, offered up repeated prayers and celebrated the sacred mysteries. A crowd of his Brothers stood round him, praising, worshipping and blessing Almighty God, who has done great things over all the world.[23] The whole people swelled the volume of praise to God, and paid their dues of holy thanksgiving to St Francis in honour of the Most High Trinity. Amen.

All this took place in the city of Assisi in the second year of the pontificate of Pope Gregory on the seventeenth day before the Kalends of August.[24]

NOTES

1 Ezekiel 28.14.
2 Compare Hebrews 1.3.
3 Philippians 3.10.
4 Compare the words of the *Exultet*, sung on Holy Saturday: 'Though the fire was divided into flames [to light other fires], the lending of its light does not involve a diminution of its own strength.'
5 Louis IX, later canonized.
6 A pun (*Franciscus . . . francus*) which is difficult to reproduce convincingly in English.
7 See John 3.29.
8 Another play on words: the cardinals are here called *cardines mundi* = 'the hinges of the world'.
9 On 27 March 1228 the party of Frederick II rebelled against the pope.
10 Pope Gregory left Rome on 20 or 21 April 1228.
11 The Curia was at Rieti between 25 April and 10 May 1228.
12 About 25 miles north of Rieti. See Part I, Chapter I, Note 1.
13 The Poor Clares at the monastery of St Paul near Spoleto.
14 The pope was in Assisi from 26 May to 12 June 1228.
15 1 John 1.1.
16 John of Brienne, crowned King of Jerusalem in October 1210, and Emperor of Constantinople in 1228. He later entered the Franciscan Order.
17 The church of St George.
18 Ecclesiasticus 50.6–7.
19 1 Timothy 1.15.
20 Ottaviano Ubaldini de Mugello, who was to be made a cardinal by Innocent IV in 1244.
21 Cardinal Riniero Capocci de Viterbo, a Cistercian. Among other things, he composed the hymn *Plaude turba paupercula* for Lauds on the feast day of St Francis.
22 Perhaps one of the hymns in St Francis' honour had already been written. Pope Gregory himself composed several.
23 Ecclesiasticus 50.24.
24 That is, on 16 July 1228, the ninth Sunday after Pentecost. Celano was surely an eyewitness.

Chapter II

The Miracles of St Francis

In the Name of Christ, Here Begins an Account of the Miracles of Our Most Holy Father

127 Humbly imploring the grace of our Lord Jesus Christ we will now under his guidance give a brief but accurate account of the miracles which were recounted in the presence of his lordship Pope Gregory (as described above), and made known to the people, both to inspire and foster the devotion of men today and to strengthen the faith of those to come.

THE HEALING OF CRIPPLES

On the very day that the hallowed and holy body of St Francis was buried (like a most precious treasure, anointed rather with celestial unguents than with earthly spices), a girl was brought to his tomb whose neck for a whole year had been so horribly bent that her head seemed joined to her shoulder and she could only look up sideways. But after she rested her head for a while on the tomb in which the precious body lay, she could immediately straighten her neck through the merits of the great saint, and her head returned to its natural position. The girl was so absolutely amazed at the sudden change in herself that she took to her heels in floods of tears. And where her head had pressed on her shoulder during her long illness, it had left a kind of hollow.

128 In the region of Narni there was a boy whose leg was so bent back that he could not walk at all without the aid of two sticks. He was a beggar and had suffered from this terrible infirmity for some years, and he did not know his own father and mother. But by the merits of our most blessed father Francis, he was cured of his affliction so completely that he could

get about freely wherever he wanted without the support of sticks, and this he did, praising and blessing the Lord and his saint.

129 A man called Nicholas, a citizen of Foligno, had a crippled left leg and suffered excruciating pain. In his efforts to recover his health he spent so much on doctors that he overstretched himself and ran up debts he could not repay. At length, when nothing the doctors did helped him in the slightest and he was in such terrible pain that his repeated screaming kept the neighbours from sleeping at night, he made a vow to God and St Francis[1] and had himself taken to the saint's tomb. After he had prayed all night before Francis' tomb, his leg was straightened and he went back home without a walking stick, in transports of joy.

130 There was also a young boy who came to the tomb of St Francis with a leg so bent that his knee seemed attached to his chest, and his heel to his buttocks. His father was wearing sackcloth and his mother was mortifying herself cruelly for her son's sake. But suddenly the boy was cured so completely that he was able to run through the streets of the city, hale and hearty again, giving thanks to God and St Francis.

131 In the city of Fano[2] there was a cripple whose legs were covered with ulcers and were doubled back so badly that his heels touched his buttocks, and they gave off such a stench that the attendants at the hospital simply refused to take him in and keep him there. But soon, through the merits of our most blessed father Francis, whose mercy he implored, to his great joy he was cured.

132 There was a girl from Gubbio who had crippled hands and for a year now had completely lost the use of all her limbs. Hoping for a miraculous cure, her nurse carried her with a wax image[3] to the tomb of the most blessed father Francis.

And after she had been there for around eight days, suddenly the girl's limbs were all restored to normality, and she was considered fit to go back to her former occupation again.

133 Another boy, too, from Montenero[4] lay for several days before the doors of the church where the body of St Francis is at rest.[5] He was unable to walk or sit because from the waist down he was quite paralysed and had lost the use of his limbs. But one day he got into the church and after touching the tomb of St Francis went out again completely sound and healthy. The little boy himself used to say that while he was lying at the tomb of the glorious saint, a young man appeared before him above the tomb dressed in the habit of the Brothers; he had some pears in his hand and called to him, and offered him a pear and urged him to get to his feet. The boy took the pear from him and told him: 'Look, I am crippled. I cannot possibly get up.' He then ate the pear he had been given and reached out to take another pear the young Brother was offering him. The young man again encouraged him to get up, but the boy felt as incapable of movement as ever, and did not do so. But as he was reaching out and taking the pear, the young Brother took his hand, led him out of the church and then disappeared from sight. The boy, seeing that he was well again and in perfect health, began to shout aloud and show everyone he met what had happened to him.

134 A woman from the hill town of Coccorano[6] was carried to the tomb of St Francis on a wooden pallet. She was so paralysed that she had lost the use of every part of her body except her tongue. But after only a short while before the saint's tomb she got to her feet, completely cured.

Another citizen of Gubbio brought his crippled son in a basket to the saint's tomb and he was restored to him in perfect health. The boy had been so severely crippled that his legs were doubled back on themselves and all but wasted away.

135 There was a citizen of Narni called Bartholomew, an extremely poor and needy man, who once fell asleep under the shade of a walnut tree and on waking found himself so crippled that he could not walk at all. The affliction grew gradually worse until one whole leg and foot became emaciated, bent and withered, and he had no sensation there – he could feel no knife cutting his flesh or fire burning it. But St Francis, true lover of the poor and father of all the needy, appeared to him one night in a vision and told him to go to a certain bathing-place where he would cure him of his sickness, because he felt such great pity for him. But when he awoke, not sure what to do, Bartholomew told the bishop of his vision, exactly as it had happened. The bishop urged him to go in haste to the place St Francis had named, then made the sign of the cross over him and blessed him. So Bartholomew, propped up on a stick, dragged himself along there as best he could. And as he was making his way there, worn out with the effort, a pathetic sight, he heard a voice saying to him: 'Go in the peace of the Lord. I am the one to whom you made your vow.' Then, as he approached the bathing-place, it being night-time he strayed from the path; and again he heard the voice telling him that he was not going the right way, and directing him towards the bathing-place. When he reached it and entered the water, he felt one hand on his foot and another on his leg, gently stretching it. At once he was cured and he leapt from the water praising and blessing the omnipotence of the Creator, and blessed Francis his servant, who had so graciously granted him a miracle. For he had been crippled and a beggar for six years, and he was of a ripe old age.

OF THE BLIND WHO RECEIVED THEIR SIGHT

136 A woman named Sibyl, who had been blind for many years, was brought to Francis' tomb in utter dejection. But after recovering her sight she returned home beside herself with joy.

A blind man from Spello[7] who had lost his eyesight long ago recovered it at the tomb of the saint.

Another woman from Camerino[8] had entirely lost the use of her right eye. Her parents placed a piece of cloth the blessed Francis had touched on her blind eye, and after making a vow, they gave thanks to God and St Francis for the recovery of her sight.

A similar thing happened to a blind woman of Gubbio who made a vow, and to her great joy she could see every bit as well as she had before.

A citizen of Assisi had been blind for five years. During Francis' lifetime this man had been an intimate acquaintance of his, and he used always to recall their friendship when he prayed to the saint, and after touching his tomb he was healed.

A man called Albertino of Narni had been totally blind for about a year, and his eyelids hung down to his cheeks. He made a vow to St Francis, recovered his sight, and got himself ready at once and went to visit the glorious tomb.

OF THOSE POSSESSED BY DEMONS

137 There was a man in the city of Foligno named Peter who, when on his way to visit the shrine of Blessed Michael the Archangel[9] (either because of some vow he had made or to do a penance imposed on him for his sins) came to a certain spring. Being tired and thirsty after his journey, he drank some of the spring water; and he could only think that there had been demons in what he had drunk, because for three years he was tortured by them, and he did the most terrible things, things horrible to see and horrible to relate. But, as the devils raged within him and tormented him cruelly, he went to the tomb of St Francis and there, by a clear and obvious miracle, when he touched the sepulchre he was cured.

138 There was a woman in the city of Narni who was subject to fits of madness, and when she was out of her

mind she did and said the most terrible things. Then finally St Francis appeared to her in a vision and said: 'Cross yourself.' And she replied: 'I cannot.' So the saint himself made the sign of the cross on her and so rid her of her madness and the demons that plagued her.

Similarly many men and women who were tormented and plagued in various ways by devils and deluded by their wiles were wrested from their grasp by the singular merits of the holy and glorious father. But because people of that kind are often victims of self-delusion, we will not dwell on the matter. Let this brief account suffice, and let us pass on to things of greater importance.

OF THE SICK SAVED FROM DEATH; OF THOSE WITH TUMOURS, DROPSY, ARTHRITIS, PARALYSIS AND VARIOUS OTHER AILMENTS

139 A baby boy called Matthew, from the city of Todi[10] lay in bed for eight days as if dead; his mouth was clenched tight, he had lost his sight completely, the skin of his face and hands and feet had turned as black as soot, and everyone gave him up for dead. But after his mother made a vow to St Francis he recovered with incredible speed. He vomited up putrid blood through his mouth and people thought he was bringing up his intestines, too, but his mother knelt and humbly called on the name of St Francis, and as she rose from her prayer the boy began to open his eyes and to see again, and to suck at her breasts. And soon afterwards the black skin fell away, his flesh regained its normal colour, and he got better again and recovered his strength. As soon as he began to get well his mother asked him: 'Who saved you, my son?' And he answered with a lisp: 'Ciccu, Ciccu.' Again she asked: 'Whose servant are you?' and again he answered: 'Ciccu, Ciccu,' for because he was an infant he could not speak properly, and this was his way of shortening Francis' name.[11]

140 A young man who was staying in a mountainous region had a bad fall and lost his power of speech and the use of all his limbs. He neither ate nor drank anything for three days, and lay there like a corpse and was thought to be dead. But his mother did not seek the assistance of any doctors: she begged St Francis to save her son. And when she had made her vow he was restored to her safe and well, and she at once began to glorify the Saviour's omnipotence.

Another boy, named Mancino, was at death's door and everyone utterly despaired of his recovery; but after he summoned the strength to call on the name of St Francis, he recovered immediately.

A young boy from Arezzo named Walter suffered from a chronic fever and was in agony from a double abscess. All the doctors had given him up for dead but his parents made a vow to St Francis, and in answer to their prayers he was restored to health again.

Yet another invalid who was close to death was suddenly relieved of all his suffering when he made a waxen image, and even before he had finished it he was delivered from all his suffering.

141 There was a woman who had been bedridden for several years and could neither turn nor move at all, but she made a vow to God and St Francis and was completely cured of her sickness and able to do everything she needed to do to live a normal life.

In the city of Narni there was a woman who for eight years had had a hand so withered that she could do nothing with it. At length St Francis appeared to her in a vision and by stretching her hand made it function as well as the other.

There was a youth in the same city who for ten years had been gravely ill and had become so bloated that medicine could do nothing for him. But by the merits of St Francis, to whom his mother made a vow, he at once recovered his health.

In the city of Fano there was a man suffering from dropsy whose limbs were grotesquely swollen, but by the intervention of St Francis he was fortunate enough to be completely cured of his illness.

A citizen of Todi suffered so badly from the arthritic swellings in his joints that he could neither sit nor rest even for a moment. The pain caused by this disease was so acute that it gave him constant fevers, and he seemed no more than a living corpse. He called in doctors, had one bath after another, and took a variety of medicines, but none of these things brought him any relief. Then one day in the presence of a priest he made a vow to St Francis, hoping that he might give him back his health. And when he had finished his prayer to the saint, he soon saw that he was completely well again.

142 A woman who lay paralysed in the city of Gubbio invoked blessed Francis' name three times and was freed of her infirmity and made well again.

There was a man named Bontadoso who suffered such pain in his feet and hands that he could not move or turn in any direction. When he could no longer eat or sleep, a woman came to him one day with some advice: she suggested that if he wanted to be rid of his infirmity in no time at all he should make a solemn vow to St Francis. In absolute agony Bontadoso replied: 'I do not believe he is a saint.' But the woman kept urging him to do as she said, until finally he gave in and made the following vow: 'I vow myself to St Francis, and I will believe he is a saint if he cures me of my illness in three days.' And by the merits of St Francis he was soon cured, and could walk and eat and sleep, and gave glory to God for his deliverance.

143 A man had been seriously wounded in the head by an iron arrowhead which had gone through the socket of his eye and stuck there, and there was nothing the doctors could do to help him. Then in humble devotion he made a solemn vow

to St Francis in the hope that he might be cured by his intercession. While he was sleeping a while, St Francis told him in a dream
to have the arrowhead removed through the back of his head.
Next day he had this done, just as he had been told in the dream:
the arrow came out without much difficulty and he was relieved
of his pain.

144 A man called Imperator who lived in the hill town of
Spello had for two years suffered from a rupture so
severe that all his intestines were pushing through his lower parts.
For a long time he had not been able either to put them back or
hold them in place, and he had to have a truss made to keep them
inside his body. He kept consulting doctors, begging them to
relieve the pain, but he had hardly enough to keep himself from
day to day and they demanded a fee he simply could not afford.
Finally, giving up all hope of them helping him he turned to
heaven for aid and, whether indoors or out of doors, wherever
he was he began humbly to invoke the merits of St Francis. And
so it happened that in a short space of time he was completely
restored to health through God's grace and the merits of St Francis.

145 A Brother living under the obedience of our Order in
the Marches of Ancona was suffering terrible pain
from a large ulcer in the lower abdomen (according to some
sources, it was in the region of his ribs) and the infection was so
acute that doctors had despaired of curing him. Then he begged
the minister[12] under whose obedience he was living to grant him
permission to visit the place where St Francis was buried, believing
that through the saint's merits he would be blessed with a cure.
But his superior forbade him to go, fearing that the exhausting
journey through snow and rain (for it was that time of year) might
cause his condition to deteriorate. The Brother was annoyed at
being refused permission, but one night St Francis appeared at his
side and said: 'My son, stop worrying about this: just take off the
fur coat you have on and throw away the plaster and the bandage

over it and observe your Rule, and you will be well again.' When the Brother got up next morning he did exactly as Francis had told him, and as a result he was soon giving thanks to God for a miraculous recovery.

THE CLEANSING OF LEPERS

146 At San Severino in the Marches of Ancona there was a young man named Acto whose whole body was covered with scabs, and who was considered by doctors and everyone else as a leper.[13] All his limbs were swollen and bloated, and because of the distention and dilation of his veins his vision was badly distorted. He could not walk, poor boy; he just lay on his sickbed all the time breaking his parents' hearts. His father was tortured each day by the cruel suffering his son had to endure, and he did not know what to do. Finally it came into his heart solemnly to commend his son to St Francis, so he said to him: 'Son, St Francis is famous everywhere for his miracles. Why not vow yourself to him and see if he deigns to cure you of this illness?' And the youth replied: 'I will, father.' So his father had some paper brought and with it measured his son's height and girth. 'Up you get, son,' he said, 'and vow yourself to St Francis. When he grants you a cure, you shall take him a candle as big as you are every year for the rest of your life.' The boy did as his father told him; he got to his feet as best he could, and clasping his hands together began humbly invoking the compassion of St Francis. And sure enough, when he took the piece of paper in his hand, and said his prayer, he was instantly cured of his leprosy, and he stood upright and began happily to walk about, glorifying God and St Francis.

In the city of Fano there was a youth called Buonuomo who was thought by all the doctors to be paralysed and a leper. He was solemnly consecrated to St Francis by his parents and subsequently cured of his leprosy and his paralysis, and regained perfect health.

147 At Citta della Pieve there was a very poor beggar boy who had been totally deaf and dumb from birth. His tongue was so small and deformed that after repeated examinations his doctors thought it had been cut off. One evening he went to the house of a native of the town called Mark and begged him for shelter. He used sign-language, as dumb folk do, leaning his head on one side, and resting his cheek against his hand to indicate to the man that he wanted to stay the night there. The man gladly took him into his house, and was happy for him to stay there, because the boy proved to be a useful servant. He was a bright lad, because although he had been deaf and dumb from the cradle, he could understand by sign-language everything he was told to do. One night when the boy was waiting on them at supper, the man said to his wife: 'I should consider it the greatest miracle if St Francis enabled this lad to speak and hear again.'

148 He added: 'I vow to the Lord God that if St Francis deigns to work this miracle, for love of him I will cherish this boy as my own and provide for him for the rest of his life.' And – wonder of wonders – no sooner were the words out of his mouth than the boy spoke. He said: 'St Francis lives!' Then, looking about the room he pointed and said: 'I see St Francis standing up there! He has come to make me speak again!'[14] Mark was overcome with joy; he rose from the table, and told everyone he could find what had happened. Everyone who had known the boy before, when he could not speak, ran to the house to see, and were astounded at the change, and gave humble praise to God and St Francis. The boy's tongue grew until its size was quite normal and he began to form words properly and to speak as if he had always been able to do so.

149 Another boy called Villa could not speak or walk, so his mother made a waxen image as a votive offering

and took it most reverently to St Francis' resting-place. When she returned home she found her son walking and talking.

A man living in the diocese of Perugia had completely lost the power of speech; he kept his mouth permanently open, gaping horribly, and was in great pain, because his throat was badly swollen and inflamed. When he came to the resting-place of St Francis and tried to climb the steps to the tomb, he brought up a great deal of blood. Then, completely relieved, he began to speak again, and was able to close and open his mouth normally.

150 There was a woman who suffered such a terrible burning sensation in her throat that her tongue dried up and stuck fast to her palate. She could neither speak nor eat nor drink. She was given plasters and medicines, but nothing brought her any relief from her infirmity. Finally, not being able to speak, she made a vow in her heart to St Francis, and suddenly with a crack the flesh of her mouth was loosened and a small round stone issued from her throat which she took and showed everyone she came across, and she was soon quite well again.

There was a young man in the city of Greccio who had lost his hearing, his memory and his speech, and could not understand or grasp anything he was told. But his parents, who had great faith in St Francis, made a vow to him on their son's behalf with humble devotion, and when the vow had been fulfilled, through the favour of the most holy and glorious father Francis, he was once again fully endowed with all the senses he had lacked.

To the praise, glory and honour of Jesus Christ our Lord whose kingdom and empire endure firm and immovable for all ages to come. Amen.

NOTES

1 In the following Paragraphs a number of different kinds of vows are made, sometimes to St Francis alone, sometimes to God and St Francis. Vows fall into two main categories: the first is a solemn promise to do something as an offering to God in return for some favour. The majority of the present cases are of this type. (The specific

content of each vow is not made clear, but Albertino in Paragraph 136 seems to have promised to make a pilgrimage to St Francis' tomb. In Paragraph 146 a yearly offering of a candle is promised.) The second category is a commitment to religious profession: in return for, or in thanksgiving for, a favour, someone solemnly vows to become a monk or nun. (In some cases here, where the vow is made specifically to St Francis, rather than to 'God and St Francis' this might be taken as meaning entering Francis's own Order.) In the Middle Ages, parents sometimes destined their child for a monastic life in gratitude for some blessing. Nicholas in the present instance (Paragraph 129) might have made such a vow, also Bontadoso in Paragraph 142 and the unnamed man in Paragraph 143.

2 Fano is 30 miles north-east of Ancona on the Adriatic coast.

3 The precise form of the wax images referred to here and in Paragraphs 140 and 149 is uncertain: they may have been images of St Francis, or perhaps in some cases models of the parts of the body affected by disease, and left at the saint's tomb in the hope of a cure.

4 There are two Monteneros in Umbria: one near Perugia, the other near Todi.

5 That is (or was when Celano was writing), St George's. See Part II Chapter X note 5.

6 Coccorano is about seven miles north of Assisi.

7 Spello is about five miles south-east of Assisi.

8 Camerino is rather more than 20 miles east of Assisi.

9 This is the shrine on Monte Gargano in Apulia where the Archangel Michael appeared in the time of Pope Gelasius (AD 492–6).

10 Todi is about 23 miles south of Perugia. It was the birthplace of Jacopo de' Benedetti (c. 1250–1306), a poet and mystic who is said to have written the *Stabat Mater*.

11 The name 'Francisco' was and still is commonly shortened to 'Cecco'; the little boy could only manage 'ciccu'.

12 The minister under whose obedience the Brother lived would be the Minister Provincial, who had authority over all houses of the Order within a given area.

13 On lepers see Part I Chapter VII note 4.

14 I have omitted two short sentences which interrupt the flow of the narrative and in themselves do not make much sense. [And he added: 'But what shall I tell the people?' Mark replied: 'You shall praise God and save many men.']

Epilogue

———

151 We have included only a little of all that might be written about the many miracles of our most blessed father Francis, and leave those who wish to follow in his footsteps the task of seeking after the grace of new blessing,[1] so that he who by his word and example, life and teaching, has most gloriously regenerated the whole world may ever deign to shower new heavenly gifts upon the minds of those who love the name of the Lord. I entreat all who read these words, for the love of the poor crucified one and the holy wounds of his crucifixion which St Francis bore on his body – I beg all who see them and hear them to remember me, a sinner, before God. Amen.

Blessing and Honour and All Praise Be to God the Only Wise, Who Always Works in All Things Most Wisely to His Glory. Amen.

NOTE

1 The author leaves it to future friars to pray for the new miracles that are bound to occur through the intervention of a saint who, when alive, did so much to regenerate the world through all he said and did.

———

Index

Numbers in brackets refer to notes.